Books a

FOR LOVE
AND MONEY
NEW ILLUSTRATION

Liz Farrelly and Olivia Triggs
Laurence King Publishing

Contents

Illustration is here to stay

Since the turn of the millennium, there has been much trumpet-blowing to herald a so-called renaissance in illustration, in both design magazines and books, which set out to showcase the best contemporary work. Illustration was 'the next big thing'; it was the result of innovative technology in the hands of maverick newcomers; or, alternatively, it demonstrated a back-to-basics revival of handcraft skills.

That search for a 'hook' is over; illustration, as a form of visual communication, has gone way beyond trends. For this new generation of illustrators, there is no need to make a simplistic either/or choice of materials or techniques, to adopt partisan preferences for traditional, analogue tools and materials or for digital means – computers, scanners, cameras. If one attitude links these practitioners, it is a pragmatic approach to image-making; whatever is best for the job, whatever is at hand, they will use it. After all, a tool is a tool; media and materials, likewise. It's not that 'anything is good enough'; it's more like 'everything is possible'.

The work in this book demonstrates an extraordinary diversity of approaches. When making the selection, we asked contributors to describe their creative methods. What we discovered was that, alongside a high degree of technical innovation, in the greater scheme of things the idea was paramount. If five illustrators scan a hand-drawn pencil sketch and manipulate it in Photoshop, there is no one predictable outcome. Choice and invention are at the root of the commercial application of illustration because, as freelance suppliers, illustrators aim to offer the commissioner something unique, something that only they can do.

Another reason for the diversity of approach and output may be down to influences; these illustrators have grown up with computers, digital communication, multiple channel television and the Internet, affording them unprecedented access to visual imagery and design from all eras. Pop culture images, for example, feature strongly as inspiration, be they from sweet wrappers, kids' television shows or music videos. Similarly, the history of image-making offers a canon of creative ancestors – artists, illustrators or designers. As part of their process, the illustrators featured in this book research, compile, edit, collage, alter and recombine. We asked contributors to reveal what they collect. The results crossed over between 2D and 3D, vintage and futuristic, objects and images, and came in myriad formats, including downloaded from the Internet, films on DVD, antiquarian books and vintage comics.

Today, visual stimulation in the form of images, patterns and animation (the emotive sibling of illustration) pervade all media across the commercial, communication, entertainment and political arenas. This maelstrom provides an ever-evolving cultural backdrop for the work of these young, contemporary illustrators.

The Illustrated World

King of the wheat-paste poster, Shepard Fairey (who created the subcultural meme 'Obey the Giant') turned Barack Obama into an iconic image, Brand Obama, which spoke directly to a young constituency and is fast achieving legendary status, à la Che Guevara. Also during the US presidential campaign, Ron English, the master of lowbrow and a godfather to street art, morphed the candidate into a portrait of President Lincoln; 'Abraham Obama' underlines an often-cited political metaphor and assumes the gravitas of a present-day icon.

In the world of advertising imagery, both still and moving, both the 'enfant terrible' agencies and the more established sets of initials are happy to suggest illustrated solutions to their biggest brands. Telecom company Orange's outdoor advertising campaign by Mother showcased the work of young illustrators and designers, realized as 48-sheet billboards high above our city streets, while a television spot by Bartle Bogle Hegarty for the soap-powder brand, Persil, featured a beautifully crafted children's pop-up book.

Similarly, multimedia creative Michel Gondry, working for Motorola, created a painted, collaged, quick-change cardboard world; Airside, for Virgin Trains, envisaged a happy red (corporate colour) world with animated dancing frogs; and McFaul, for Havaianas, attached a giant flip-flop to a painted mural in New York City. The invention and adaptability of illustration within advertising, across media, scale and location, continues to be proven, again and again.

As a means of communication, whether the message is news and opinion or simply fun, illustration delivers. While the design and editorial teams at publications as diverse as the Guardian, The Drawbridge and Illustrated Ape in London, WAD in Paris, and the New York Times in the USA, among many others, strive to bring the best of illustration to their readers, on a larger scale, the success of animated music videos has introduced new legions of fans to the power of the drawn image. Since the turn of the millennium, animation studio Shynola has been wowing audience and critics alike with an unpredictable mixture of cute-meets-sinister characters romping around psychedelic dystopias, with clients ranging from UNKLE to Radiohead buying into Shynola's skewered imaginings.

At the cinema, animation is no longer a niche entertainment but is attracting audiences of all ages, be it with Pixar's Oscar-winning blockbuster WALL-E, with its mix of inventive styles; the sheer patterned dynamism of DreamWorks' Kung Fu Panda; the fantastical otherworldliness of myriad films by Japan's Studio Ghibli; or the UK's Aardman Animations, with its surreal/kitsch take on a strangely familiar reality.

Back in the world of real things, illustration features on the objects we use every day. Illustration has covered books and music packaging since the mid-twentieth century. Today's book designers not only commission images, but often create their own illustrations, employing an expanded palette of visual means to connect with diverse audiences. Chip Kidd, designing for Knopf, HarperCollins and Doubleday, references his eclectic influences, from comic-book memorabilia to classic Modernist design. Working for Penguin, David Pearson has been instrumental in the repackaging of collected volumes, turning type into image for the series Great Ideas, abstracting nature for Great Loves and quoting figurative styles of a bygone era for Great Journeys.

The illustrated book is experiencing a renaissance, prompted by the explosion of street art as a publishing genre. Illustrators are producing their own books; Paul Davis's Us & Them uses the most economic of means to describe the 'special relationship' between Americans and Brits. Meanwhile, Lawrence Zeegen has leveraged a career teaching illustration into a series of books advising on technical, aesthetic and conceptual issues.

While the music industry worries that it is losing ground to the download, some stellar examples of image-led packaging still make it to the racks. Sanna Annukka's folkloric surrealism graces releases by the band Keane, while Tom Hingston Studio (responsible for many high-profile covers during the past decade) regularly commissions illustrators, such as Siggi Eggertsson for Gnarls Barkley's The Odd Couple, and Cecilia Carlstedt for Faze Action's Broad Souls.

In another design sphere, illustrated decoration, applied to 3D objects, is transforming our homes into atmospheric environments. Lighting and tableware by Tord Boontje, for Habitat in the UK and Target in the USA, feature laser-cut fronds and blooms alongside transfer-printed creatures and landscapes, all conspiring to make home a more magical place. Meanwhile, Spanish designer Jaime Hayon covers plates, vases, walls, shop and restaurant interiors with bold, expressionist strokes and calligraphic messages.

On the world stage, the fashion industry is a main defining factor in the aesthetic zeitgeist of an era. Today's fashion is a riot of eclecticism – pattern, colour and image – but with clear lines of influence travelling both ways, from illustration, graphic design and street art to fashion, and back, in the form of collaborations and commissions. We endlessly remake ourselves, using fabrics and garments to apply images and pattern to our bodies. Back in the eighteenth century, patterned cottons stoked demand for new fashion and spurred on the Industrial Revolution. In the twentieth century, since the inception of ready-to-wear, image has been mechanically applied to garments, by means of print, weave, knit, embroidery and embellishment. Some recent examples of image-led fashion include the all-over comic-bold graphics at Bernhard Willhelm; eclectic, clashing geometries at Marc Jacobs; Serum VS Venom's, graphite-toned knitwear; and Miu Miu's metallic mosaics and spray-painted prints.

Graphic designers too are getting in on the pattern-making craze; sisters Nicole and Petra Kapitza have developed 'pattern fonts', which allow the user to build intricate, unique patterns simply by typing on a computer keyboard. Their 'people silhouette fonts' work in the same way; featuring drawings of individuals snapped on the streets of the world's cities, these image banks are a useful tool for all designers and image-makers.

Alongside the traditional areas where illustration shines, new means are emerging to further disseminate work. Thanks to the ease of setting up e-commerce sites, young designers and illustrators are selling their wares online. With a boost in eco-awareness, the reusable canvas tote bag has become a welcome addition to our urban landscape; a leitmotiv you shouldn't be caught without. Emblazoned with graphics and illustrations, these bags act like a moving canvas, and are perfect for mixing messages and self-promotion.

Meanwhile, a resurgence of DIY attitudes has prompted many illustrators to set up their own screen-printing studios. Add to that a proliferation of giclée printing technology and you have a grass-roots movement, producing genuinely affordable art. Whether hand-printed or digital, limited edition or one-off, prints by designers and illustrators are being sold online, in guerrilla galleries and at impromptu exhibitions staged by creative co-operatives. These no-holds-barred forums are producing dynamic results for an enthusiastic audience.

WELCOME TO THE SELECTION

These days, it seems, 'more is more'; our lives are full of illustration, pattern and colour, thanks to illustrators of all stripes stepping up to add their mark to the mêlée. Unsurprisingly, the contributors to this book are dabbling their toes in all of the above activities, some of which are documented here. With limited space, only a handful of projects could be featured for each contributor, so please visit their websites for more information.

As an intended showcase for some of the world's most innovative young illustrators, this book could only ever be a personal selection, albeit made by a team of three, so as not to foreground any one person's taste (that team being creative director Michael Dorrian and authors Liz Farrelly and Olivia Triggs). Selection criteria demanded that the illustrators be drawn from the widest geographical spread, the aim being to bring new talent to public attention. The contributors were also judged on the calibre of their clients and their media exposure in exhibitions and magazines, which we felt demonstrated their intent on building long-term careers as professional practitioners. We think that this selection offers a glimpse of the best illustration now, and for the future.

Liz Farrelly

REFERENCES

aardman.com
airside.co.uk/work/projects/virgintrains
bartleboglehegarty.com/#/europe/our-work/41
blog.mcfaul.net
copyrightdavis.com
davidpearsondesign.com
direct.motorola.com/hellomoto/razr2/razr2makingof
dreamworks.com
goodisdead.com
guardian.co.uk
hayonstudio.com
hingston.net
kapitza.com
marcjacobs.com
miumiu.com
motherlondon.com
nytimes.com
obeygiant.com/prints/inauguration-print
openspace.bscientific.org
pixar.com
popaganda.com
sanna-annukka.com
shynola.com
studioghibli.net
svsv.net
thedrawbridge.org.uk
theillustratedape.com
tordboontje.com
wadmag.com/wadmag
zeegen.com

CHRISSIE ABBOTT

What did you study?
Illustration at London College of Communication.

What inspires you?
People, music, colour, memories, seeing
new things, the past, the future.

What do you collect?
Old photographs.

What is your favourite way of working?
I like to collage found images, and mix them
with drawing and painting, and use Photoshop.

Where do you work, play and travel?
Everywhere.

In My Mind I'm Clapping 2008
Personal project; hand-drawing, collage,
mixed media.
© Chrissie Abbott

'Self-promotional image for
my first solo exhibition at the
Old Shoreditch Station in London.'

Little Boots 2008
Client: Little Boots
Music packaging and identity; collage, digital.
Exhibited at 'It's Nice That' in London.
© Chrissie Abbott

'This ongoing project for the solo musician
Little Boots includes the artwork for CD and
vinyl releases as well as an evolving identity.'

Vetika 2008
Personal project; hand-drawing, collage.
© Chrissie Abbott

'Limited-edition, A3-sized print, part of a
series that is inspired by the apocalypse.'

2K 2008
Client: 2K by Gingham
T-shirt design; hand-drawing.
© Chrissie Abbott
'I was commissioned to design three
T-shirts for the client's Artists series.'

MORE THAN REAL

EDA AKALTUN

What did you study?
Graphic Design and Communication Design at Central
Saint Martins College of Art and Design, London.

What inspires you?
Family photographs from the 1950s and 1960s, Jim
Jarmusch films, Marc Caro and Jean-Pierre Jeunet's
sense of humour, Moholy-Nagy, Paul Auster's detective
stories, Kafka.

What do you collect?
Old photographs, old textbooks, vintage architecture
and fashion magazines; all of which make my studio
very dusty.

What is your favourite way of working?
It changes, from beginning in a sketchbook to starting
up the computer. I try to go back to analogue methods,
using etching or screen printing, as I think this adds an
element of atmosphere to my work. I'm obsessed with
layering, whether it's on the screen-printing table or in
Photoshop. I also have a 'library' of textures and I don't
feel that an illustration is finished without the inclusion
of some sort of organic element.

Where do you work, play and travel?
I work in west London and play in east London. I travel
to the Far East, and recently my favourite destination is
Japan. I'd like to visit Arizona and the Grand Canyon.

Metamorphosis 1, 2, 3 2007
Personal project; collage,
two-colour screen print.
© Eda Akaltun

'Series of seven images in response to
Franz Kafka's short story <u>Metamorphosis</u>.'

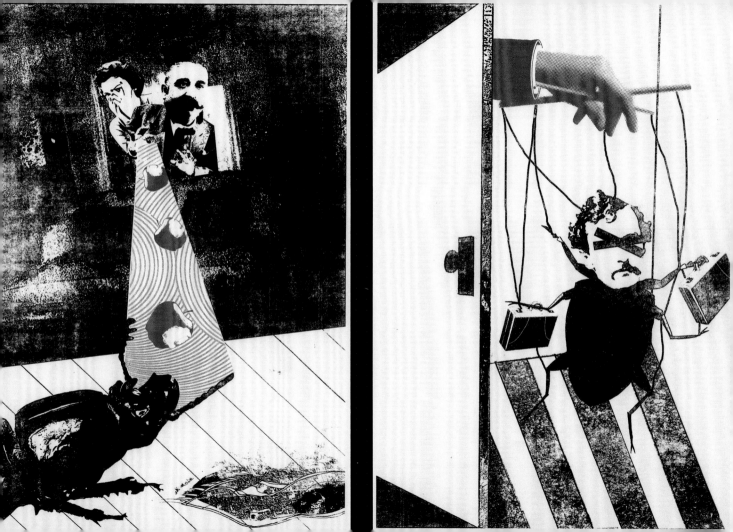

Surveillance 2008
Personal project; mixed media,
digital collage.
© Eda Akaltun

'From a series of A3-sized
images dealing with different
aspects of surveillance.'

Gut instinct 2008
Client: Australian Financial Review
Magazine illustration; digital collage.
© Eda Akaltun

'This article looked at the positive and the negative issues
around using "gut instinct" as a way of making business
decisions. This image was also a limited-edition print,
and was exhibited at "Illustrative" in Zürich.'

Takayo Akiyama

What did you study?
Graphic Design at Musashino Art University, Tokyo, and Communication Design at Central Saint Martins College of Art and Design, London.

What inspires you?
Friends, music, films, partying all night and then going to the park, daydreaming, conversations with old people and young kids.

What do you collect?
Photocopies from my library research; small souvenirs from my travels.

What is your favourite way of working?
Researching at the library and then going to the pub. I like to work with stories, and make comics and moving images. I use Rotring pens (0.13 to 0.7), Saunders Waterford paper and my drawing board.

Where do you work, play and travel?
I'd like to work in a bigger studio, with a screen printing press. I play locally, in east London. I'd like to travel to Mexico.

Twins 2007
Client: Illustrated People
Fashion collection illustrations; hand-drawn, pen, computer.
© Takayo Akiyama

'For Spring/Summer 2008, the theme was "psychedelic summer and sex", so I drew naked twins. Used for advertising and T-shirt designs.'

The Siamese Twins 2006
Client: Frédéric Cambourakis,
Edition Cambourakis
Poster, cover, comic book; originally
screen printed on sugar paper, reprinted
on coated paper.
© Takayo Akiyama

'This is my first comic book, and was
originally made for my MA final project.
Now it's been published and exhibited at
Festival International de la Bande Dessinée
d'Angoulême, France. The main characters
are Siamese twins called Daisy and Violet,
who work in a pub as pianists, and who find
love in this monstrous world. The colour
palette is inspired by a children's nursery-
rhyme book from 1925.'

Pablo Alfieri/Playful

What did you study?
Graphic Design at the University of Buenos Aires;
I'm a self-taught illustrator.

What inspires you?
Music and sounds, space and the stars,
love and my girlfriend.

What is your favourite way of working?
My method has four steps: think, draw some sketches,
create using the chosen technique, end result. I prefer
to make digital illustrations, and that's always the final
part of my process.

Where do you work, play and travel?
I love to travel to Europe, and enjoy the culture and
art in cities such as London, Paris and Barcelona.

A Sound Supreme,
Children Of The Idiom 2008
Client: Phil Chang
Book illustrations; custom typography, digital.
© Pablo Alfieri

'These images were commissioned by
Phil Chang, who asked a group of artists
to each illustrate a track from his album.
These were collected into an A5-sized
book sold with the album.'

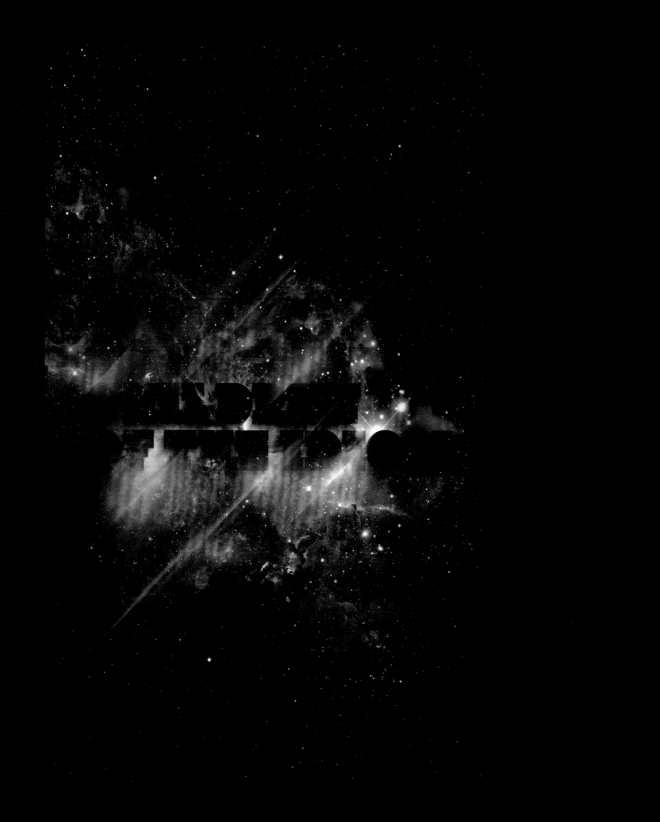

GEO THE PL
ME PINT AY 2008
TRY SERIES FUL

Geometry Series 2008
Client: The Pint Series
Limited-edition postcard set; digital.
© Pablo Alfieri

'I used masks to create the geometric
forms, then illustrated the galaxies,
coloured the image and added
the typography.'

GEO THE PL
ME PINT AY 2008
TRY SERIES FUL

Materia 2008
Client: Materia
CD cover; Cinema 4D,
Adobe Illustrator, Photoshop.
© Pablo Alfieri

'This is the first album by
Argentinian band Materia.'

Low Poly 2008
Personal project; hand-drawing,
Cinema 4D, vector graphics.
© Pablo Alfieri

'Limited-edition poster set.
This is a personal experiment
using low polygons in 3D.'

Beautiful/Decay 2008
Client: Beautiful/Decay
T-shirt design; photography, digital.
© Pablo Alfieri

'The clients wanted a collage with
galactic images, skulls and typography;
the end result is my mix, including
photographs I shot.'

What did you study?
Graphic Arts at Liverpool School
of Art and Design.

What inspires you?
Originality.

What do you collect?
Graphics annuals, old postcards,
books and ornaments.

What is your favourite way of working?
I make quick pencil sketches to work
out the composition, and use the
computer to draw and collage.

Where do you work, play and travel?
Work: my studio. Play: the park.
Travel: everywhere.

 Res 2008
Client: Res
Magazine illustration; digital.
© Emily Alston/Emily Forgot

'This image for a Swedish travel
magazine illustrated an article
about future modes of transport'

Tall Tale 2008
Personal project; digital.
Exhibited by Thick and Thin at
Mother in London.
© Emily Alston/Emily Forgot

Limited-edition A1-sized prints from a
series of 13 images loosely based on
'ytales. Each piece aims to capture the
untold moments of a familiar tale.'

MICHELE ANGELO/ SUPEREXPRESSO

What did you study?
Fine Art, Visual Communication,
Industrial Design.

What inspires you?
The handcrafted approach to design;
the contrast between modern tools
and classic, humanist techniques.

What is your favourite way of working?
I like to work at night; I experiment
across many design fields to find a
new solution that fits each project.
I'm not interested in following trends.

Where do you work, play and travel?
Barcelona and Italy.

Milk on Mars 2008
Personal project; oil paint, Adobe Illustrator,
Photoshop, canvas.
Exhibited at a solo show, 'Cosmolove', at
Libenter, in Mantova, Italy.
© Michele Angelo/Superexpresso

'This series of images was inspired by
space, intergalactic travel and love, and
I asked what if milk were found on the
planet Mars instead of water. I used this
opportunity to experiment with paint,
mixing it with digital media; I also played
with typography and words.'

Funghi Porcini 3 2008
Personal project; Adobe
Illustrator, Photoshop.
Exhibited at a solo show, 'Cosmolove', at
Libenter, in Mantova, Italy.
© Michele Angelo/Superexpresso

'I started drawing a set of organic numbers
for the anniversary of an electronic music
club, and three is my favourite so far. I also
love elephants and mushrooms, so this
illustration pays homage to the "elephants
on parade" sequence from Disney's film
Dumbo, which I first watched as a child.'

Justine Ashbee

What did you study?
Textile Design at the Rhode Island School of Design.

What inspires you?
The colour spectrum, the ocean, ancient cultures that built structures in line with the cosmos.

What do you collect?
Tea, patterns, geometric forms, images of strata found in nature, and images of underwater sea life.

What is your favourite way of working?
I love the immediacy of using marker on paper and on walls, and I allow whatever to occur within simple parameters.

Where do you work, play and travel?
The ocean and the woods; I like to work in silence and be open to the whispering universe.

Phases 2007
Photographer: David Clugston
Commissioned drawing; marker, paper.
© Justine Ashbee

A Certain Kind of Sensation 2006
Photographer: David Clugston
Personal project; marker, paper.
Exhibited at the Angle Gallery, Seattle.
© Justine Ashbee

'From a series of drawings exploring
unseen, intuitive nature.'

Unfurl, Unfold, Untold 2007
Client: Andrio Abero
Personal project; marker, paper.
© Justine Ashbee

'From a series of commissioned
drawings exploring things that we
feel but cannot see; a trace of the
invisible, flowing wave patterns.'

Jesse Auersalo

What did you study?
Graphic Design at the University of Art and Design, Helsinki.

What inspires you?
Don't be scared, don't hide, be true to your ideals; people will recognize that.

What is your favourite way of working?
I enjoy working at home, listening to music. Before I start I like to make sure I know exactly what I'm going to do; it's not easy to change crap into gold.

Where do you work, play and travel?
It's good to keep moving; there's a lot to see.

**Oh My God You Look Good Can
I Touch Oh It's Fake** 2008
Client: Kasino A4
Editorial illustration; digital.
© Jesse Auersalo

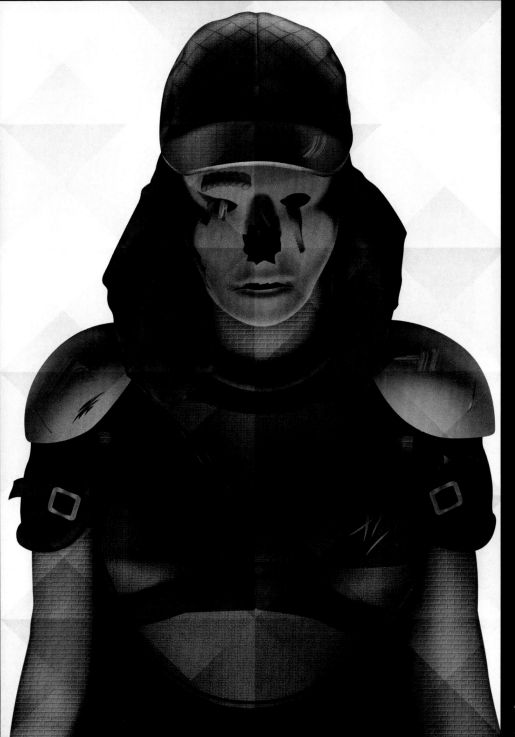

Dollhouse Riot 2008
Personal project; digital.
Series of posters exhibited at
'Night On Earth' at the Museum
of Contemporary Art in Shanghai
© Jesse Auersalo

Mind Fuck 2008
Client: <u>Kasino A4</u>
Editorial illustrations; digital.
© Jesse Auersalo

Vicarious Bliss 2008
Client: Club Misf*ts
Gig poster; digital.
© Jesse Auersalo

Matt Didemus (Junior Boys) 2008
Client: Club Misf*ts
Gig poster; digital.
© Jesse Auersalo

Clemens Baldermann/ Purple Haze Studio

What did you study?
Fine Art, Painting and Graphic Design.
I'm a self-taught illustrator.

What inspires you?
Everything. I share a studio with C100,
so I exchange ideas with Christian Hundertmark,
which is inspiring.

What do you collect?
In the back of my sketchbook is a wallet containing
snippets and finds, from sketches, drafts and notes,
to stickers, photos and labels. Once in a while I'll
compose them into a collage.

What is your favourite way of working?
My design philosophy is: believe in the process, be
authentic, be brave, have fun, and then the direction
or genre follows on. I like to work across disciplines,
as energy emerges from the contrasts. Generally,
I start with a pencil sketch on paper. Then I'll cut
or rip out the significant drafts, and stick them
on the wall for another look.

Where do you work, play and travel?
I work in a very nice studio, close to parks and the
River Isar in Munich. My favourite leisure activities
are riding my BMX, meeting friends and hiking in
the Bavarian mountains.

'Blues and Reds' by **Justine Electra** 2006
Client: Cityslang Records
Illustrations for record cover and vinyl labels; collaged
hand-drawn and printed elements, ink, watercolour, pencil.
Sleeve printed four-colour, labels printed spot-colour.
© Clemens Baldermann/Purple Haze Studio

'The idea was to use collage to visualize the musical style,
which is somewhere between folk, blues, electro and pop;
inspiration came from the collages of painters
such as Cy Twombly and Robert Ryman.'

Licht 2 2006
Client: <u>Licht 2</u>, Die Krieger des Lichts
Contribution to A2-sized poster magazine,
and limited-edition poster for the launch
exhibit of <u>Licht 2</u>, at Gallery Tristesse Deluxe
in Berlin.
Editorial image; vector graphics, printed matter,
printed spot colours with fluorescent ink.
© Clemens Baldermann/Purple Haze Studio

Selekta! 2006–8
Client: Selekta!
Flyers and posters for a club night; collages combining
vector graphics, ink, screen printing and printed matter
printed using spot colours, metallic and fluorescent inks.
© Clemens Baldermann/Purple Haze Studio

'I wanted to create a new visual language to communicate
this genre of electronic music and the club night.'

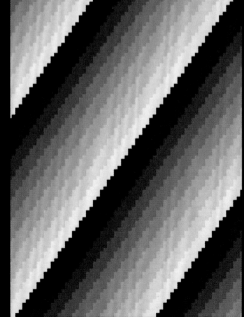

Siren 2008
Illustrations for Siren, a handbound,
limited-edition zine. Collages combining
photography, vector graphics, spray paint,
ink, screen printing, monochromatic print
on various coloured paper stock.
Issue one, launched at an exhibition
at Soda Books in Munich.
© Clemens Baldermann/Purple Haze Studio

'The aim was to create a platform, a
playground for work in text and images, and
a "nice leaf through" of eclectic content, with
the help of guest contributors
Purple Haze Studio, C100 Studio,
Bob Sanderson and Florian Seidel.'

HOLLY BIRTLES

What did you study?
Photographic Arts at Westminster University.

What inspires you?
Theories of phenomenology, visual awareness and
perception, most importantly shapes, textures and
organic objects. I often use mechanical imagery;
its uncanny resemblance to nature inspires me.

What do you collect?
Books on plants and animals, obscure plants,
paper textures, a diverse range of tape.

What is your favourite way of working?
Photographic montage; a combination of darkroom
and film-based imagery, plus paints, textures, papers
and digital editing.

Where do you work, play and travel?
I often visit industrial locations to find discarded
mechanical objects, and gardens to find obscure
plants. I go to as many locations as possible; you
never know what you'll find, and every place is
inspiring in a very different way.

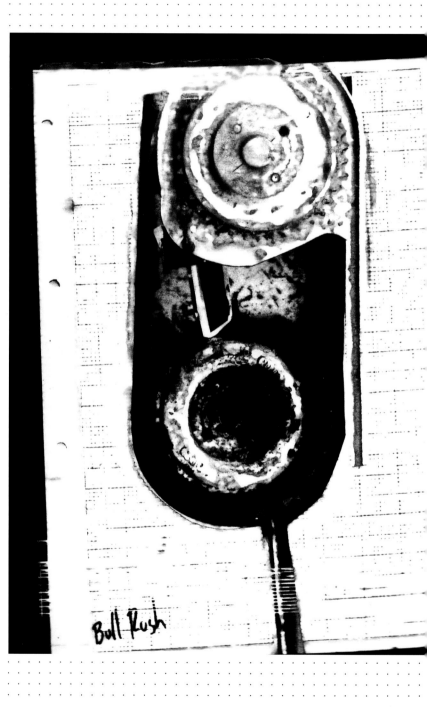

Bull Rush 3 2008
Personal project; photographs, paper, paints.
One-off print, series of 55 plants, printed
in book form as Mechanical Plants:
Pre-explosion, and exhibited at The Truman
Brewery in London.
© Holly Birtles

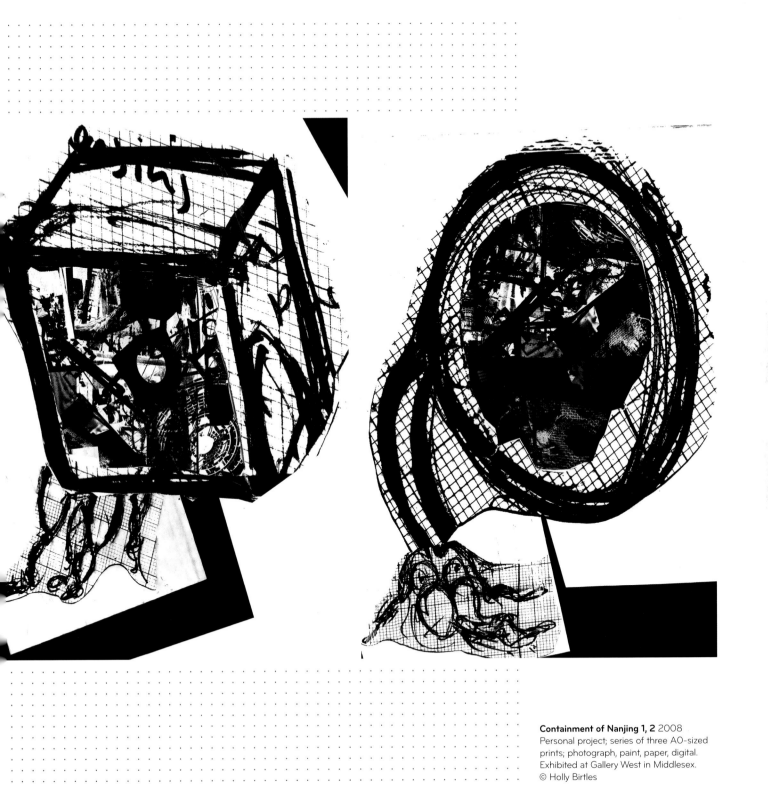

Containment of Nanjing 1, 2 2008
Personal project; series of three A0-sized
prints; photograph, paint, paper, digital.
Exhibited at Gallery West in Middlesex.
© Holly Birtles

45

What did you study?
Graphic Design at the University of Buenos Aires.

What inspires you?
I try to look at everything with fresh eyes; right now I'm reading about and researching Pre-Columbian cultures.

What do you collect?
I love nature, and have lots of different plants in my house. I also collect antique books.

What is your favourite way of working?
I try to change my method for every new piece of work; but I always start the process with a very fast sketch, just to explore the general concept. I like to mix materials, such as pencils, ink, markers, spray paint, and compose the final piece digitally.

Where do you work, play and travel?
I'm always working; every place I go I have a little block and pencil with me. At home I play with my dog; and I love to travel by train.

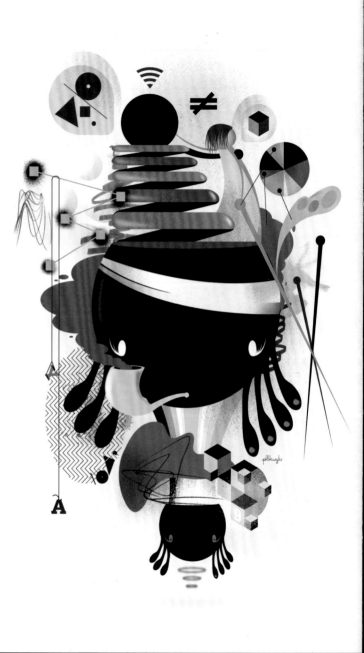

Guru Dream, El Despabilador 2008
Personal project; pencil, marker, spray
paint, digital.
Limited edition, exhibited at 'Illustrative'
in Zürich.
© Pablo Bisoglio

'This series came from a difficult time
in my life, and I've tried to express that.'

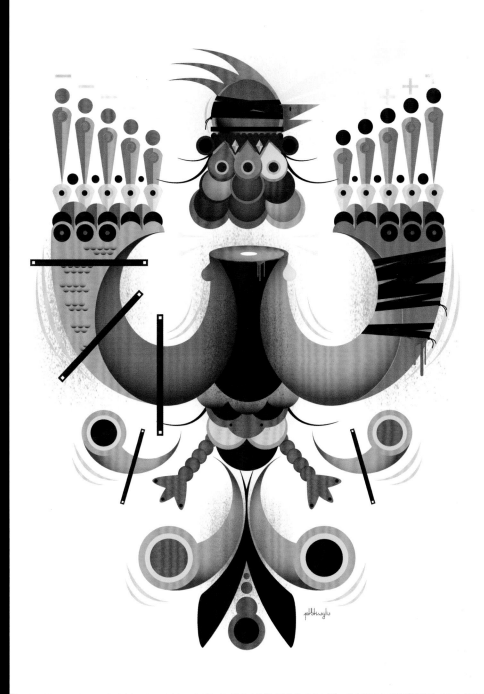

Sebastian Bissinger/BANK™

What did you study?
Graphic Design, Photography and Illustration.

What inspires you?
Content, illustration and design on found objects
and packaging, and the streets.

What do you collect?
Tons of printed ephemera.

What is your favourite way of working?
A mix of drawing and digital image-making; changing
settings, adding layers and transparency, switching
between positive or negative, altering colours.

Where do you work, play and travel?
Work, play and travel should be all the same.

International Gigolo 2007
Client: International Gigolo Records
Record packaging; various
computer applications.
© Sebastian Bissinger/BANK™

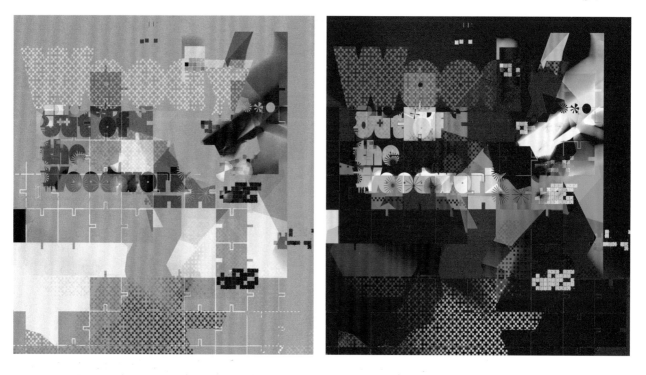

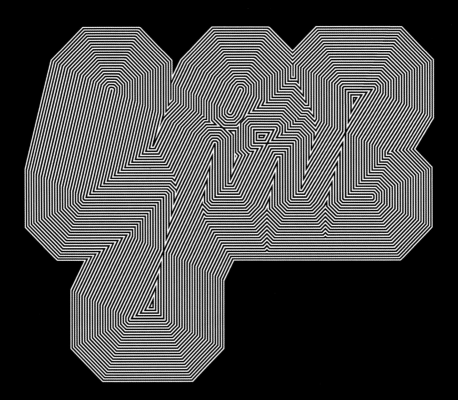

Girl 2008
Client: EW Records
Vinyl sleeve; digital.
© Sebastian Bissinger/BANK™

'After we'd used the title of the release, Girl,
to create an op-art effect, the client chose
a totally different solution.'

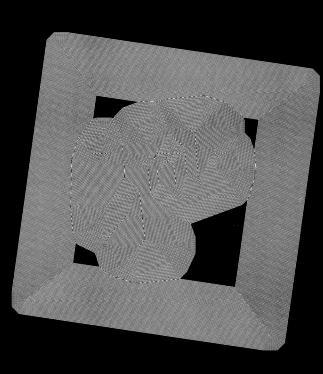
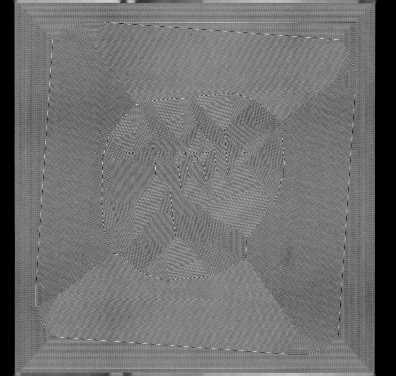

What did you study?
Graphic Design and Multimedia at
ESAAT Roubaix and ENSAMAA Paris.

What inspires you?
Immateriality; feelings, atmospheres,
sensations, sensuality, eroticism.

What do you collect?
Little pieces of pictures, details
that I find interesting.

**What is your favourite way
of working?**
I like to explore different tools, work
with my hands, draw, build, cut, and
manipulate with a computer. I'm
working in print, as I like paper and
it's such a concrete medium.

Where do you work, play and travel?
If you're relaxed, design becomes
a kind of game or trip.

Caress 2005
Personal project; crayons, gouache,
photography, glue, paper.
Exhibited at La Petite Fabrique
in Caen, Normandy.
© Laure Boer/BANK™

'Series of one-off posters that investigates
the tension between two bodies, just
before they touch. It was important for me
to create that erotic energy by working
with physical materials.'

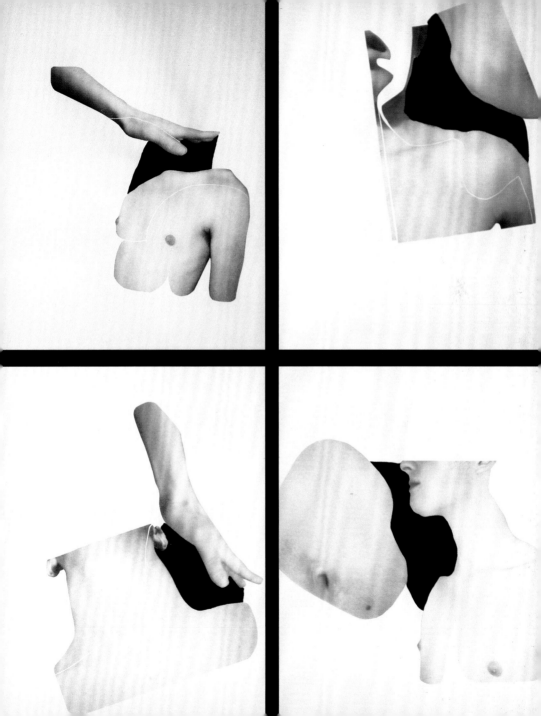

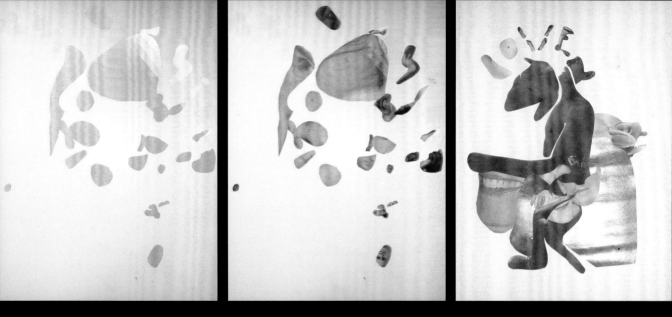

Love 2008
Personal project; found imagery, digital.
© Laure Boer/BANK™

'Series of images using clipped fragments
from newspapers and old postcards, mainly
faces, bodies, expressions, colours and
textures; by combining these elements
I create new atmospheres.'

CHRIS BOLTON

What did you study?
Graphic Design.

What inspires you?
Everyday things, people
and surroundings.

What do you collect?
Unique, ephemeral objects.

What is your favourite way of working?
I start with a strong idea, work with
pen and pencil on paper, and move
through to the final conception,
usually on computer.

Where do you work, play and travel?
Work: Helsinki. Play: ice hockey.
Travel: wherever and whenever possible.

Lindstrom and Prins Thomas 2005–7
Client: Eskimo Recordings/NEWS NV
Collaborator: Juha Nuutti
Music packaging; vector illustrations
recreated in wood.
© Chris Bolton

'This album imagery came from the fact
that the band was Norwegian; the Beatles'
song, Norwegian Wood gave me the idea
for the wooden images. The decision to use
animals came from the abundance of forests
in Norway, so I asked the guys to pick a few
creatures, but not the typical reindeer!'

'Escapements' by Petar Dundov 2008
Client: Musicman Records/NEWS NV
Vector illustration for album cover.
© Chris Bolton

'The typographic illustration of interlocking
cogs was directly inspired by the
clockwork-related title'.

Lindstrom & Prins Thomas
Turkish Delight
EP

Lindstrom & Prins Thomas
Mighty Girl
EP

Lindstrom & Prins Thomas
Boney M Down
EP

Lindstrom & Prins Thomas
Nummer Fire Ep
EP

James Bourne

What did you study?
Illustration at the University of Plymouth.

What inspires you?
Structured society forces me to escape
through my drawings.

What do you collect?
I like to find things that make me curious, so
that I can create ideas about what they are.

What is your favourite way of working?
Drawing with Fineliner pens and rendering
with Photoshop; I also enjoy screen printing
and am still mastering that tool.

Where do you work, play and travel?
I spend nearly all my time in Birmingham;
I'm happy here but looking forward to
moving on.

Kings on a Bicycle 2008
Collaborator: Paul Roberts
Personal project; ink, digital.
Exhibited at Nowhere North Gallery in London.
© James Bourne, Paul Roberts

'The theme for this "Them Lot" group show was
bicycles; Paul and I decided to tackle the work
together as our linear styles are similar.'

Careful What You Smoke 2006
Personal project; ink, digital.
Exhibited at 'Them Lot Confessi[...]
at the Custard Factory Gallery in
Birmingham.
© James Bourne

'Series of images for a self-initiat[...]
book, Fighting Boredom, which
explores the novel ways in which
people deal with boredom.'

PAULA CASTRO

What did you study?
Graphic Design at the University of Buenos Aires
and Fine Art with Eduardo Medici in Argentina;
I'm a self-taught illustrator.

What inspires you?
Movies, pictures, stories, poems.

What do you collect?
Many things; mostly old toys and printed fabrics.

What's your favourite way of working?
Drawing by hand and then editing the work on a
computer. The pens I use are Pilot G-TEC-C4 0.4,
Plume and Aquarel. Sometimes I work in three
dimensions and with sound too.

Where do you work, play and travel?
Everywhere.

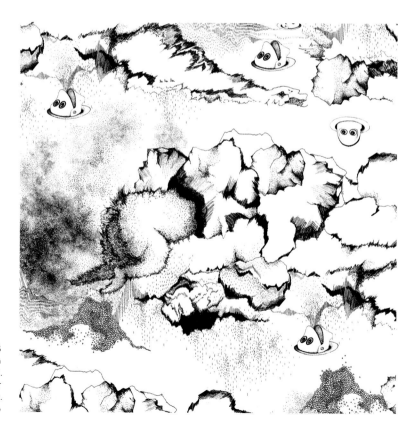

Land Escape Drawing 5, 11 2008
Personal project; ink on
paper, digital.
Limited-edition prints, exhibited at
Monotono, Vicenza.
© Paula Castro

Lines 2 2007
Client: Gas Jeans
Fashion collection illustrations;
ink on paper, digital.
© Paula Castro

'For the Spring/Summer 2008 collection,
I designed prints for clothing, the catwalk
show invitations and decorations. The
images were intended to complement
the new concept for the brand, mixing
the sensual with essentials.'

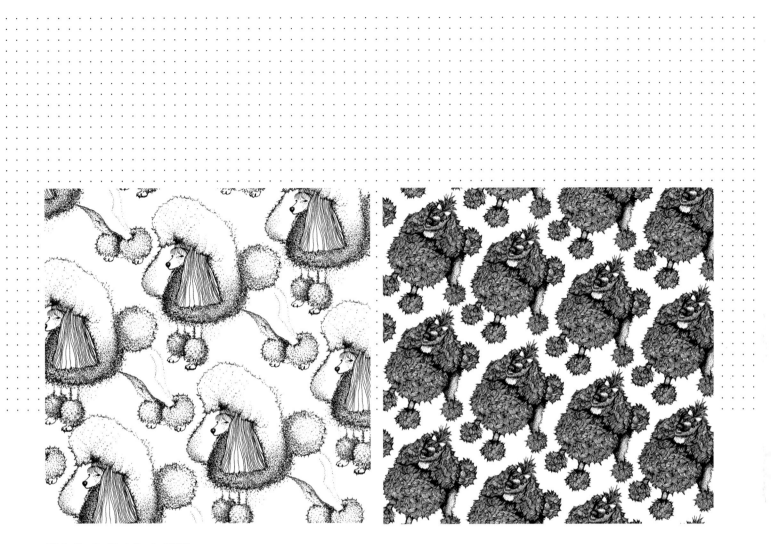

White Poodle, Black Poodle 2008
Personal project; ink on paper, digital.
Limited-edition prints, exhibited at
Monotono, Vicenza.
© Paula Castro

Pasaro, Caracol, Cones 2007
Client: Nike
Advertising poster; ink on paper.
Exhibited at the Centro Cultural Recoleta
in Buenos Aires.
© Paula Castro

'Used to publicize a 10K marathon. The
three animals represent different types of
runners: the snail for people who never run,
the birds for regular runners, the bunny
for obsessive runners. The limited-edition
poster was intended to encourage all sorts
of people to participate in the marathon.'

Ian Caulkett

What did you study?
Illustration at Norwich School of Art and Design.

What inspires you?
Music is a massive influence; I can't work without music.
I remember picking up a copy of Peter Blake's Sgt. Pepper
album sleeve when I was a kid, and being mesmerized
by it. I was really into Oasis and spent most of my time
at school redesigning their album covers, and it just
progressed from there.

What do you collect?
Records and books — I always judge a book by its cover,
it's as important as what is inside. I have also discovered a
lot of good music and literature by picking up what I think
looks good. I also collect old postcards, family photos and
photographic slides.

What is your favourite way of working?
My work is fundamentally about collage; I prefer the
physical side of things, getting my hands dirty, making
a mess. I don't generally sketch ideas out beyond simple
scribbles; I tend to visualize the outcome in my head
and hope it takes a similar form when I create it. There's
usually some digital manipulation required, and I use
different digital processes, typography and screen
printing too.

Where do you work, play and travel?
I work in and around London, between a home studio,
an office and a screen-printing studio. I play in London,
Norwich and Cambridge, and the perfect getaway is
north Cornwall.

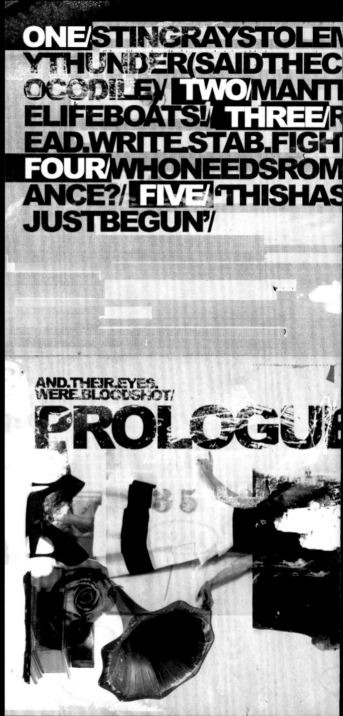

**'Prologue' by And Their
Eyes Were Bloodshot** 2007
Client: Small Town Records
CD packaging; paper and photographic
collage, typography and computer.
© Ian Caulkett

'Illustration and art direction for debut EP'

Sing the Joys Baby 2008
Personal project; screen-printed photographic
and typographic collage, old record sleeves.
© Ian Caulkett

'This limited edition features various vintage
sleeves; it's of a baby photo of me wearing
Dad's headphones; I remember listening to
old Elvis records with my Dad. This started as
an experiment with old seven-inch dust sleeves
that had lost their vinyl. I like the effect the new
ink has on the printed surface of an artefact
that is possibly older than I am.'

Pomme Chan

What did you study?
Interior Design in Bangkok; Graphic Design at the London College of Communication.

What inspires you?
Everything... living in London, transport, weather, nature, architecture, beauty and fashion.

What do you collect?
Old postcards, pictures of animals and vintage stuff from antique markets.

What is your favourite way of working?
I like to have an image in my head first, then start drawing on paper, and sometimes develop that on the computer. But mostly my work is hand-drawn. I use pen and pencil on good-quality paper and rarely use an eraser. I love the texture and smell of ink, and at the moment, felt-tip pens are my favourite way of working. Then I mix in different papers, and some collage. I like to show in galleries because then you can see the real texture of the images.

Where do you work, play and travel?
I live in London; there's something about living there that inspires my work. For play, I travel to Japan; it's amazing – a good mix of culture and technology.

Artful Dodger 2008
Client: Artful Dodger
Series of T-shirt designs; pen, pencil, collage, computer.
© Pomme Chan

'This is the first women's collection for this label; I've designed T-shirts, prints, branding and typography for Spring/Summer 2009.'

DiRTY MONEy, FiLThY RiCH.

Hide and Seek 2008
Client: Topshop
Personal project; pen, felt-tip
pen, computer.
© Pomme Chan

'Topshop asked me to design
some T-shirts. This one is about
a game that's not just for children.
As adults we still hide from some
things, and also seek other things
or people. It seemed too "dark"
for the brief, so I kept this piece
– it's one of my favourites.'

The Happy Show 2008
Client: Yen
Magazine illustrations; pen,
pencil, felt-tip pen.
© Pomme Chan

'Series of six images for the
"happy" issue. I was asked to
draw anything cheerful and
bright, and I came up with
the "happy show"; it's what the
magazine is all about – fashion,
make-up and teenage girls.'

JOHNNY CHEUK

What did you study?
Digital Media at Hong Kong Institute
of Vocational Education.

What inspires you?
Music, movies, experiences and artists.

What do you collect?
DVDs of movies.

What is your favourite way of working?
I follow my imagination; then I use pencil, ink,
watercolour, Adobe Illustrator and Photoshop.

Where do you work, play and travel?
Japan.

Stars: Edie Sedgwick, Marilyn Monroe 2008
Personal project; pen, ink,
watercolour, digital.
© Johnny Cheuk

Josh Clancy/Toothjuice

What did you study?
I'm a self-taught illustrator.

What inspires you?
Drone tapes, 909 drum kicks, hand claps, friends,
travel, Middle America.

What do you collect?
Old magazines and packaging (from the 1970s
to the 1990s), vintage games, rocks.

What is your favourite way of working?
I work fast, busting images out in Adobe Illustrator,
using the pencil tool and a Wacom tablet.

Where do you work, play and travel?
I work at my studio and get wasted at a club!

Les Coeurs 2008
Client: Beautiful/Decay
Promotional image; digital.
© Josh Clancy/Toothjuice

'Commissioned for the Artist Series,
to be used on T-shirts, advertising
and in the magazine.'

Spoon Type 2008
Personal project; digital.
© Josh Clancy/Toothjuice

'Broccoli and bubble gum arranged
around X-rays of teeth.'

What do you collect?

My large-scale projects are made from my collections – most recently, vintage matchbooks, discarded library-book covers, old magazines, and more.

What is your favourite way of working?

Although it looks obsessive, my practice is very calm and content. I find focusing on detail and repetition to be endlessly entertaining. I'm happiest with pen, paper and a pot of glue, although these can include anything from a crow quill to a ballpoint scrounged from a desk drawer. The paper I draw on ranges from vintage postage stamps to ten-feet-long strips of masking paper, to handmade cotton-rag stock.

Where do you work, play and travel?

Work and play are the same; I love living in Los Angeles and take my sketchbook everywhere, from shows at the Upright Citizen's Brigade Theatre, to movies at the Cinerama Dome, to the Farmer's Market and even a few film sets. Sometimes I miss the weather, though, and fly home to New England to dip my toes in snow.

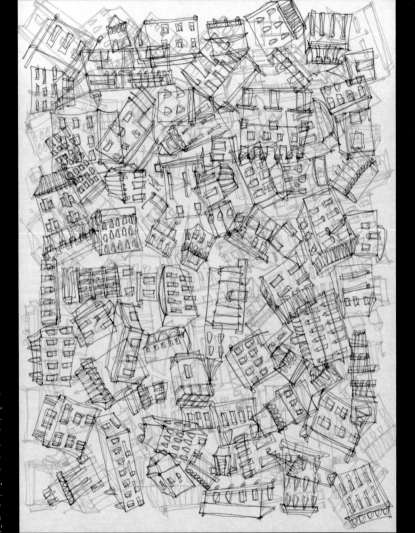

City of Industry 5 2008
Personal project; series of drawings,
ink, coloured cardstock.
© Kathryn Dilego

'City of Industry is an actual place, and the exact name I would give my own city were it ever an option. Each drawing is made using two colours of ink on cardstock, samples from a local warehouse. All the buildings are drawn in one sitting, in a loose, fluid motion that is extremely fun to do.'

The Bicentennial 2007
Personal project; hand-drawn, ink,
paper, scanned, digitally coloured.
© Kathryn Dilego

'A spot illustration of America, circa 1976

and complicated, layered work, but I don't choose between them, I combine them. The media I use depends on the work; either handmade collage, drawing or digital illustration.

Where do you work, play and travel?
I'd like to visit New York City again soon.

Promotional image; mixed-media collage.
© Frank Dresmé/21bis

'Series of illustrations that describe the future vision of this city centre; these "maps" suggest densely interwoven architecture and infrastructure, accented by inhabitants and typography.'

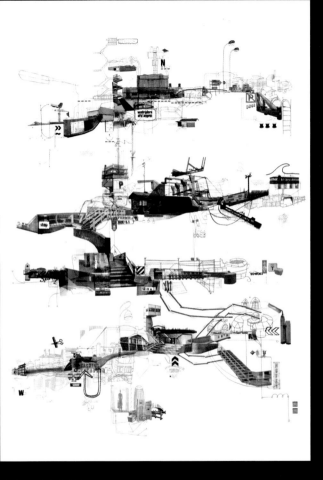

Project 360° 2007
Personal project; mixed-media collage.
© Frank Dresmé/21bis

'These four psycho-geographical maps
of Amsterdam trace personal destinations
in the city. These were published in

Tools 2007
Personal project; handmade collage.
© Frank Dresmé/21bis

'Series of images, combining a face
with the tool that person uses.'

What did you study?

I'm a self-taught illustrator.

What inspires you?

Hieronymus Bosch, Herb Lubalin,
Eero Saarinen, Oscar Niemeyer,
Otl Aicher, Francisco Goya,
David Lynch, Stanley Kubrick,
Josef Müller-Brockmann.

What do you collect?

Memories.

What is your favourite way of working?

Pen, paper and computer.

Where do you work, play and travel?

Anywhere; I'm very mobile. I have
a MacBook and a 23-inch screen,
and a digital camera that I use as
a scanner. I just worked in Brooklyn
for three months, next Stockholm,
next Buenos Aires.

Quincy J 2006
Personal project; pen, paper, computer.
© Hampus Ericstam

'A4-sized, published in WORD magazine.'

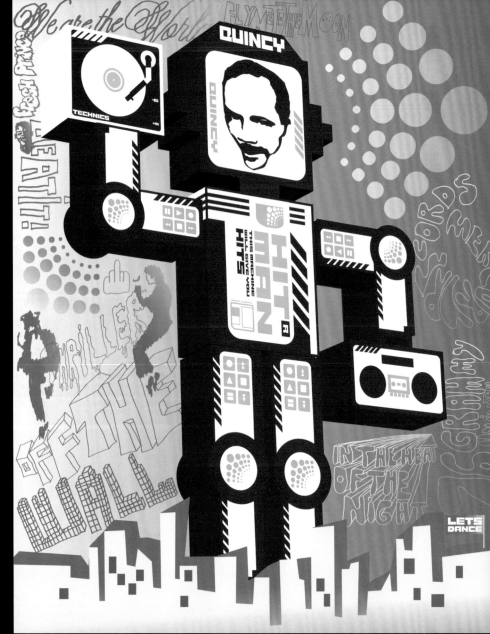

Virgin Mobile 2007
Client: Virgin Mobile
Advertising image; p
paper, computer.
© Hampus Ericstam

'From a series of six
images used in a
campaign in Europe

Dress Up 2005
Personal project; pen, paper, computer.
© Hampus Ericstam

'A4-sized illustration, published in
WAD magazine.'

Levi's Sounds 2007
Client: Levi's
Promotional illustration; pen,
paper, computer.
© Hampus Ericstam

'Used in stores, in advertising
and on CDs all over Europe.'

Gary Fernández

What did you study?
I'm a self-taught illustrator.

What inspires you?
My girlfriend, friends, travelling,
landscapes, cityscapes, shops
and music.

What do you collect?
I'm constantly moving; I don't collect,
I just save the most necessary things.

What is your favourite way of working?
I like to start with my Moleskine
notebooks, pens and pencils. I'll
define the idea, based on the brief;
then I make sketches until I find an
overview I like, and begin to refine
the elements and colours. I don't
stick to one medium; I like to try
different challenges.

Where do you work, play and travel?
Every new place provides new points
of view and experiences.

Rainy Day 2008
Client: El Duende
Magazine cover; mixed media.
© Gary Fernández

'The theme was "the danger of extinction",
so I began by thinking of the biggest
problem we have in Spain, the shortage of
water; the umbrella saves rainwater falling
from multi-coloured clouds.'

Birds 2008
Client: Computer Arts
Art director: Jo Gulliver
Magazine cover; mixed media.
© Gary Fernández

'The biggest challenge with this
cover was fitting the illustration
into the layout as there were
many different elements
to accommodate.'

Flower-head Girls 2008
Client: La Surprise

Singing Birds 2007
Personal project; mixed media.

RICARDO FUMANAL

What did you study?
Graphic Design; I'm a self-taught illustrator.

What inspires you?
Fashion, photography, pop culture.

What do you collect?
Fashion magazines, postcards, and all sorts
of found images.

What is your favourite way of working?
I research images that I find interesting, then
modify and recombine them to create new
meaning. I use pencil, coloured pencils, ink,
watercolour, paper and canvas.

Where do you work, play and travel?
I'd like to work all over the world, first in
London and Berlin.

Desprendimiento 2007
Client: Pull and Bear
Fashion catalogue illustration; pencil, ink, paper.
© Ricardo Fumanal

'From a series of ten images, which combined
photography and illustration, and were based
on Brazilian teenage culture.'

Pelo Peluca 2008
Book illustration; pencil, ink, paper.
© Ricardo Fumanal

'From a series of five illustrations for the novel
<u>Ferdinand</u> by André Gide. This is a portrait
of the story's main character.'

MELVIN GALAPON

Where did you study?
Central Saint Martins College of Art and Design, London.

What inspires you?
Friends, family and people that I admire.

What do you collect?
Stickers, coloured tape, vinyl, pens; I also bookmark
pages on the Internet, which is like collecting.

What is your favourite way of working?
Making things by hand, across as many media as I can.
I like finding new ways of working that keep me interested.

Where do you work, play and travel?
Work: in the company of friends. Play: outside.
Travel: everywhere.

Crystal Forms 2007
Personal project; hand-cut vinyl,
pencil, pen, A4-sized sketchbook.
© Melvin Galapon

'This series of six, A1-sized one-off posters
constitutes an investigation into crystal,
fragmented forms and colours.'

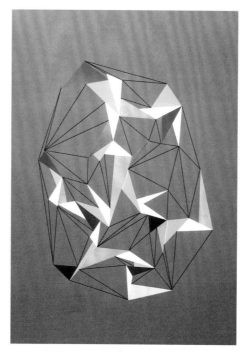

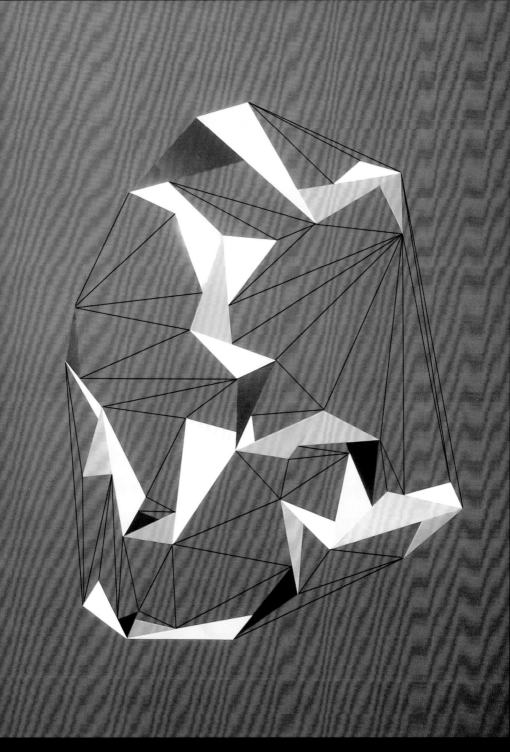

Show Off Club 2008
Client: Show Off Club
Logo design: Meirion Pritchard
Promotional posters; stickers, paper.
© Melvin Galapon

'Series of three A0-sized one-off posters,
used to decorate a venue.'

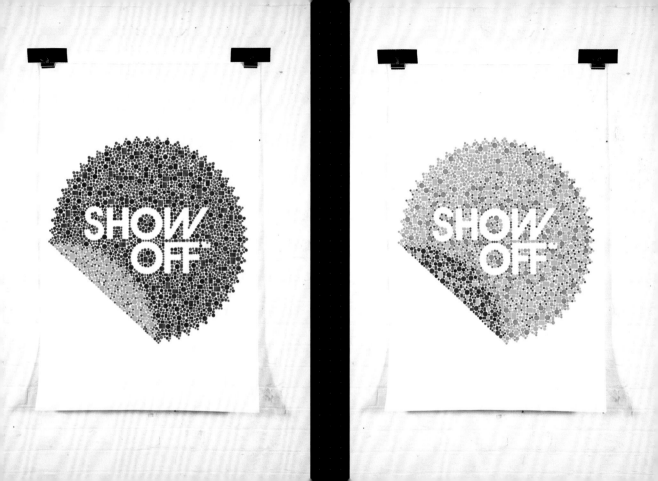

ALINA GÜNTER

What did you study?
Visual Communication at Hochschule der Künste, Berne.

What inspires you?
Memories.

What do you collect?
Shells and stamps.

What is your favourite way of working?
I like to find suitable photographs and translate them into my own personal expression, an encounter between words and visual images that melts memories. I use an Edding 1800, an Edding Profipen 0.1, pencils and coloured pencils, paper and the computer.

Where do you work, play and travel?
Work: Zürich. Play: Zürich. Travel: World.

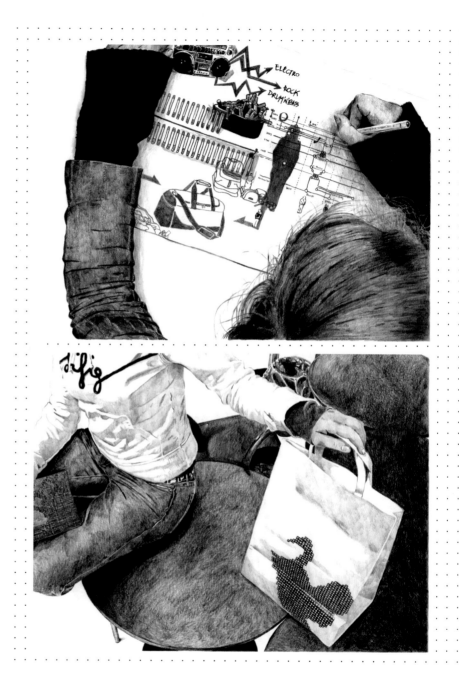

Review of the Year 2005
Personal project; pencil on paper.
© Alina Günter

'Series of seven drawings remembering a year in my life.'

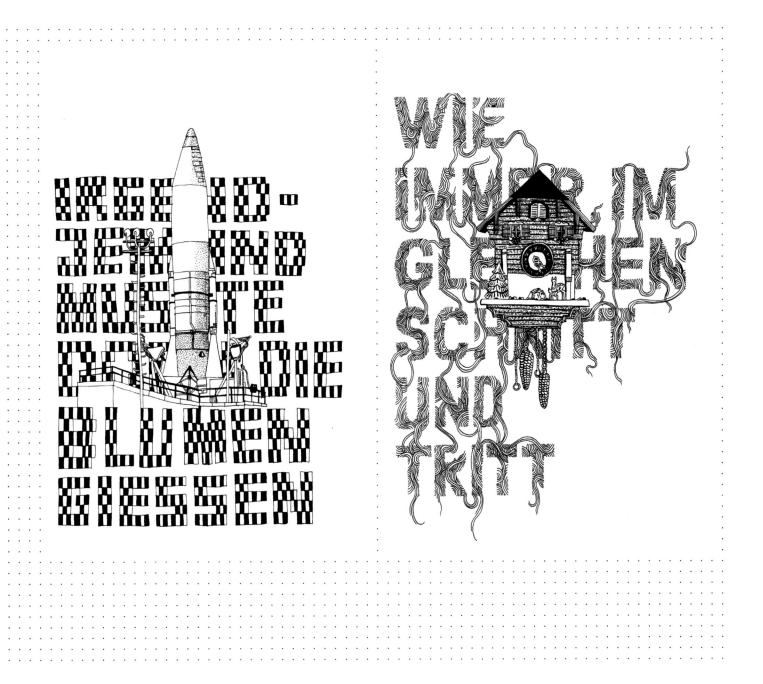

Round One 2007
Personal project; Fineliner, paper.
© Alina Günter

'Series of 13 images, aiming to associate
memories with animals and objects,
and to bring typography into the image.'

What Remains Are the Memories of the Memories 2008
Personal project; coloured pencil, Fineliner, paper.
Exhibited at 'Illustrative' in Zürich.
© Alina Günter

'Series of images about memory, containing parts
of stories of leaving. The aim is to define things that
can't be named, and express feelings and memories
that are slipping away.'

RICHARD HALL/LISTEN04

What did you study?
Graphic Design; I have always drawn,
ever since I can remember.

What inspires you?
Jimi Hendrix, Jean-Michel Basquiat, José Parlá,
hip-hop music, my family.

What do you collect?
Beer mats, hats, spray paint, trainers.

What is your favourite way of working?
Mixed media on canvas, using wood and
found materials.

Where do you work, play and travel?
I don't really get out much, I'm always working.

Let the Music Play 2007
Personal project; marker pen, acrylic, oil paint,
spray paint, collage, mixed media, canvas.
Exhibited at the Night and Day Café,
Manchester.
© Listen04

'Let the music play, just a little slower,
never miss a beat.'

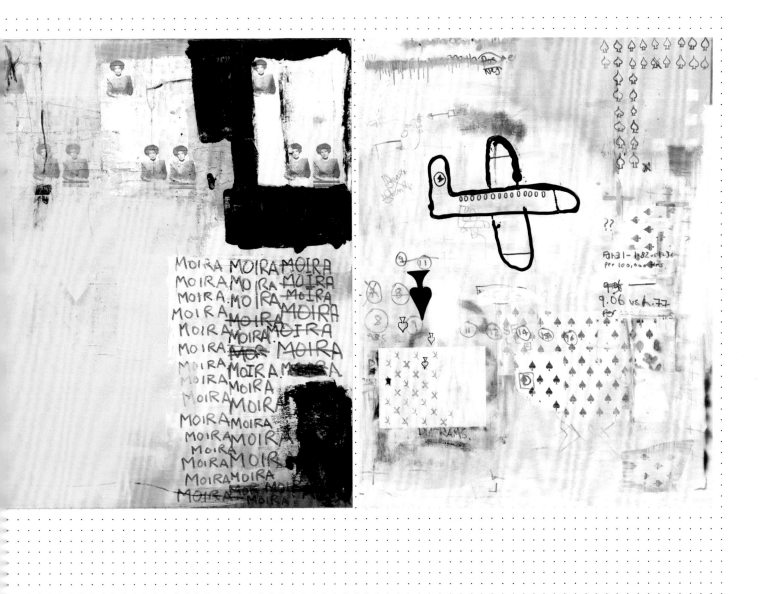

Moira 2007
Client: DJ Semtex
Personal project; marker pen, acrylic,
spray paint, collage, mixed media, canvas.
Exhibited at the Night and Day Café, Manchester.
© Listen04

'This image comments on race issues, how
barriers have been broken down, but the media
still fuels the problem. Moira is a legend!'

Plane Diagrams 2007
Personal project; mixed media, canvas.
Exhibited at the Night and Day Café, Manchester.
© Listen04

'While working in Ibiza, I experienced a series
of bad luck; a bomb scare at the airport, a car
crash, food poisoning. I didn't want to go on
that trip as I had a strange feeling that bad
stuff would happen; funny thing, intuition.'

Sara Haraigue

What did you study?
Visual Communication at Gobelins,
l'école de l'image, Paris.

What inspires you?
Photography, art, design, music,
science and people.

What do you collect?
Books, magazines, brochures,
flyers, photography.

What is your favourite way of working?
I use accident; I begin with a
small detail and work until I have a
composition. The aim of this approach
is to strip everything back to the bare
bones. I draw with Adobe Illustrator,
and build complex frameworks on to
which I stack geometric shapes.

Where do you work, play and travel?
I like to work at night; it's the best
time for me to be creative. I'd like
to live and work in London because
I love the people, the city and
the inspiration.

Electro Caramel 2008
Client: Electro Caramel
Identity for podcast; digital.
© Sara Haraigue

'Commissioned by a new radio station
specializing in electronic music. I created
this fudge-like material, a form that feels
alive and perpetually moving, just like
the radio station's exploration of diverse
music. I made a connection between the
minimalism of the form and the music.'

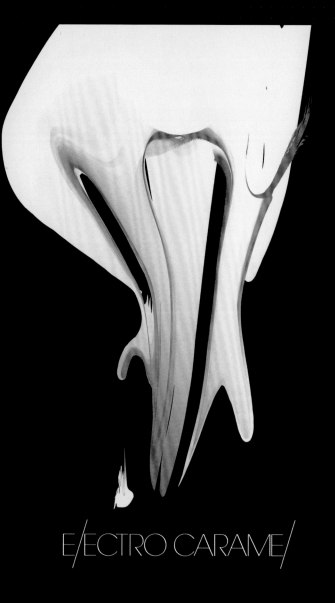

E/ECTRO CARAME/

A New Aesthetic 2008
Client: Decortica
Collaborator: Pierre Nguyen
Album cover; digital.
© Sara Haraigue, Pierre Nguyen

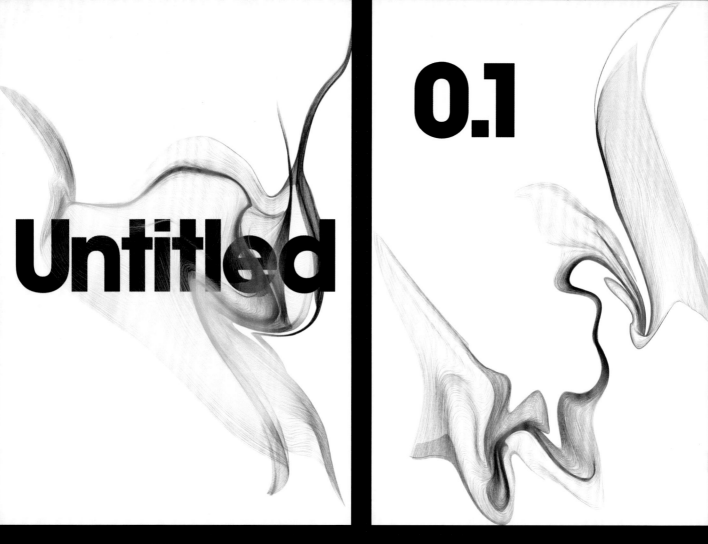

Thin 2008
Personal project; digital.

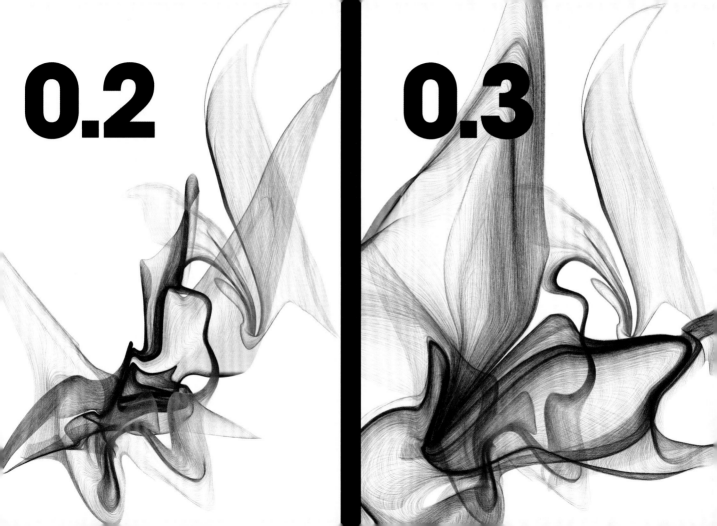

Sophie Henson

What did you study?
Graphic Design; but I knew that illustration
was more up my street.

What inspires you?
Everything, everywhere; street art, television
and the Internet are an endless source.
People's quirks intrigue me.

What do you collect?
Conversations, especially on the bus.

What is your favourite way of working?
Generally, I work with a single image as I prefer
that organic process rather than having a big
plan. I almost always start with my pencil and a
Fineliner pen, and then digitally manipulate the
doodles. I like sketchbooks and brainstorming;
and I love 2B pencils.

Where do you work, play and travel?
I love Tokyo, and Argentina is beautiful; generally,
if I have a bit of paper, a napkin or an envelope,
I can work anywhere.

Dark Summer 2008
Client: Boxfresh
Fashion illustrations; pencil, Fineliner, ink,
Adobe Illustrator, Photoshop.
© Sophie Henson

'Series of five images used on garments
for 20th Anniversary Collection, Spring/
Summer 2009. The brief was very open,
to fit the theme of "dark summer".
I'd just moved to east London, so
I wandered the streets and hung out
with the horses on Hackney Marshes;
the blimp is a little bit of artistic licence.'

Sender 2008
Personal project; hand-drawn, pencil,
Fineliner pen, ink, envelope.
© Sophie Henson

'I had a sketchbook full of doodles of
typefaces I'd seen and drawn over the
years, from vans, billboards, shop signs,
posters and packaging. I wanted to do
something with them.'

Day Job 2008
Personal project; vector graphics,
Adobe Illustrator.
Published in Computer Arts.
© Sophie Henson

'I work day-to-day, make ruthlessly
ambitious plans in my diary, but never
seem to stick to them. I have a head and
sketchbook full of things I want to do but
never get around to. This was a good
opportunity to just play around.'

Desk Job 2008
Personal project; hand-drawing,
Adobe Illustrator.
Published in Computer Arts.
© Sophie Henson

'I spent a year travelling and when
I got back home I knew that I wanted
to freelance. I spent many hours sitting
at my desk wondering how on earth
I would start, and that was the first
place I found inspiration. The Creme
Egg is particularly important.'

RICHARD HOGG

What did you study?
Fine Art at Chelsea School of Art;
I'm a self-taught illustrator.

What inspires you?
Hard work, blank paper, colours,
nature, friends, girls and other
people's work.

What do you collect?
Old fountain pens, and images
off the Internet, obsessively.

**What is your favourite way of
working?**
It varies; I draw in sketchbooks and
spend a lot of time staring into
space. Once the idea comes, the
drawing is generally quite quick. I like
to draw with old fountain pens, and
use screen printing and computers.
Occasionally I also paint giant murals.
I'd like to work more in video games
and fashion, and see my work in
nice people's houses.

Where do you work, play and travel?
I work in my studio, in Hackney,
and at home. I play in a band, go
bird-watching, walking and camping.
I don't much like foreign travel,
unless it's for work.

Acknowledgement 2008
Client: Acknowledgement
Wall mural; ink and digital artwork,
output on to vinyl.
© Richard Hogg

'Commissioned for the office of
Acknowledgement, a digital agency.
Each egg-like pot disgorges a
different category of stuff: nature,
people, mechanical parts.'

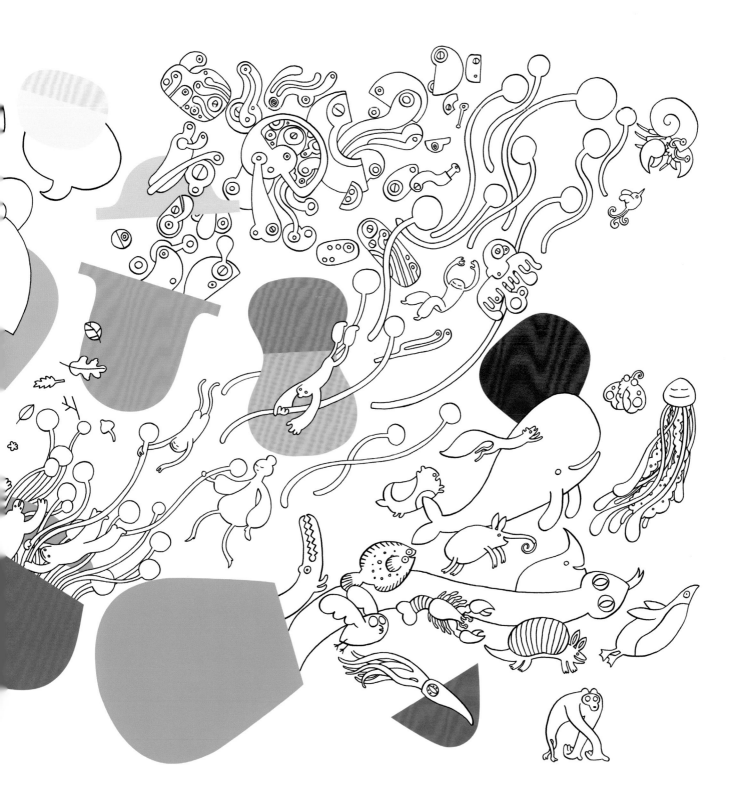

Chat-up 2008
Client: Uniqlo
T-shirt; screen print.
© Richard Hogg

'Series of three designs. This is a picture
of a man chatting up a woman; you might
try to work out what he's actually asking her...
I'm not sure.'

Tea Break 2007
Personal project; hand-drawn, ink,
coloured on computer.
© Richard Hogg

'The original drawing was A3, and
evolved into a mural for PS3/Sony at
the O2 Stadium. These two robot-like
dudes are having a tea break, while
working together in some kind of
giant, disorganized warehouse
of parts and widgets.'

Mario Hugo

What did you study?
Fine Art, Art Direction and
Communication Design.

What inspires you?
I love words, not only written, but spoken
and sung; small phrases can conjure up huge
images and I often start a piece with a title. I like
Bruno Munari's work, old films and used books
(both for their paper and as reference material).

What do you collect?
Old books and furniture, for their textures.
I like objects, but don't necessarily collect.

What is your favourite way of working?
I feel most honest with a pencil and two or
more sheets of paper; I love graphite, china ink,
fuzzy photographs, gouache and acrylic. I start
work with a book on tape and a clean slate.

Where do you work, play and travel?
I like to work in natural light; the beach
is synonymous with both play and travel.

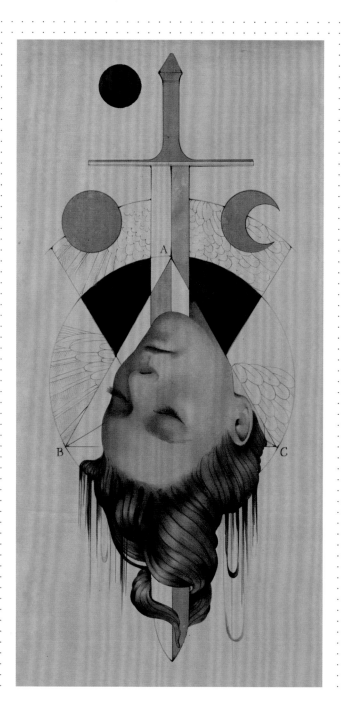

Dymphna in Effigy 2008
Client: The Fader
Magazine illustration; graphite, china ink, paper collage.
© Mario Hugo

'The image is about Saint Dymphna, a princess
who parries the sexual advances of her father,
and is decapitated by the king in a jealous rage.'

Flaunt 2007
Client: <u>Flaunt</u>
Magazine cover; pencil, china ink, gouache,
acetone-stained paper.
© Mario Hugo

'Actress Marley Shelton is depicted in a playful
composition investigating the nature of acting.'

The Unbearable Lightness of Being 2008
Film poster; mixed media.
Created for Darren Firth's travelling
exhibition, 'Now Showing' at WIWP.
© Mario Hugo

'I was asked to recreate a movie poster;
great cinematography by Sven Nykvist,
mediocre screenplay, read Milan Kundera's
book instead.'

Dolce & Gabbana 2006
Client: Giovanni Bianco, Dolce & Gabbana
Book illustration; pencil, china ink, book
pages, mixed media.
© Mario Hugo

'Created for Dolce & Gabbana's 10th
anniversary book, this piece references

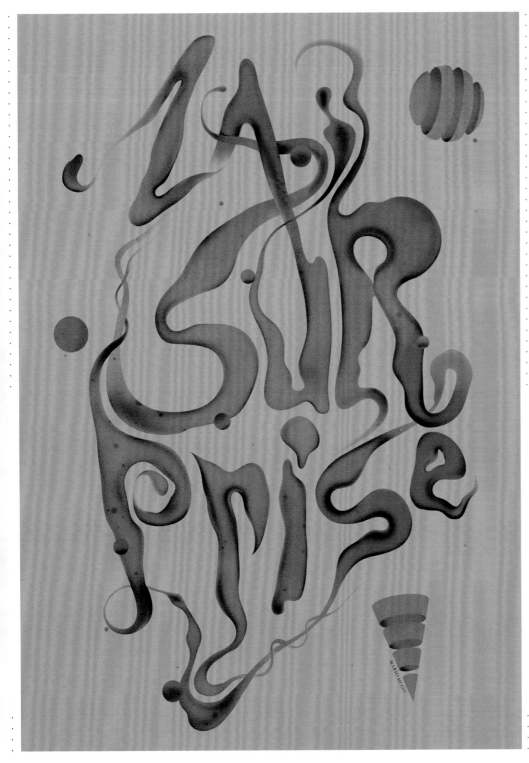

'Antigone' by Daniel Ciardi 2007
Seven-inch single cover; mixed media.
© Mario Hugo

La Surprise 2008
Client: La Surprise
Promotional image; hand-drawing,
digital, mixed media.
© Mario Hugo

'Announces the opening
of a new design studio.'

CHRISTIAN HUNDERTMARK/ C100 STUDIO

What did you study?
Graphic Design. I started drawing when I was a kid, and then began making graffiti and street art. I brought out the books The Art of Rebellion and The Art of Rebellion II, which have been called 'bibles of street art' and sold around the world.

What inspires you?
Everything that surrounds me.

What do you collect?
Other artists' work.

What is your favourite way of working?
Using my brain; I sketch the idea, scan it, and finish it on a computer. I use a pen, a mouse, spray cans, acrylic paint and canvas.

Where do you work, play and travel?
I recently had exhibitions in Barcelona and New York, and really enjoyed those, so I hope there'll be more in the future.

Zerwirk 2008
Client: Zerwirk
A4-sized posters; scanned material,
four-colour printing.
© Christian Hundertmark/C100 Studio

'A year's worth of monthly programmes for a bar and club venue, featuring an illustration on one side and listing details on the reverse.'

Ghettoblaster 2007
Client: Man Recordings
A2-sized posters for a party event.
© Christian Hundertmark/C100 Studio

The brief was to visualize the event without
resorting to the usual clichés but using
metaphors such as bass, funk, dope beats,
sneakers, Brazil and so on.'

Around the Bloc 2008
Client: Oakley
A2-sized posters; hand-drawn and

Hi Contrast 2006
A1-sized posters; hand-drawn and scanned
collage, four-colour printing.
Personal project exhibited at 'Hi Contrast'
in Zürich.
© Christian Hundertmark/C100 Studio

Marcus James

What did you study?
Illustration at Central Saint Martins College of Art
and Design, and Royal College of Art, London.

What inspires you?
Nature, human behaviour, manmade and natural
structures, fun, danger.

What do you collect?
Random fragments of skulls, dead animals and plants,
stones, press cuttings and stories, found photographs,
ephemera, vintage erotica.

What is your favourite way of working?
Drawing from life, reference and photographs.
I draw with an HB Faber Castell pencil on large
sheets of paper. I also paint and screen print.

Where do you work, play and travel?
Japan, New York, Paris, Ibiza, Scotland, India,
Morocco, and around Britain – Norfolk, the north,
Stroud, Somerset, Dalston, the park.

Skull Fuck 2008
Client: GAS
Personal project; screen print.
© Marcus James

'This series of prints uses coloured
shapes layered on to anatomical
studies, to create ambiguous sexual
poses. They were later realized as
limited-edition T-shirts.'

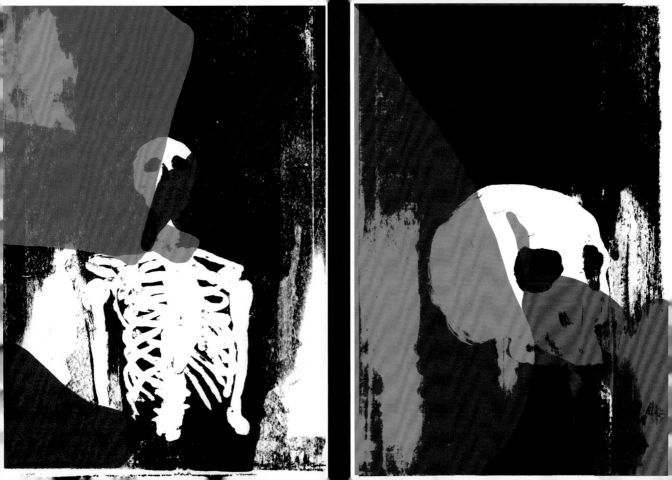

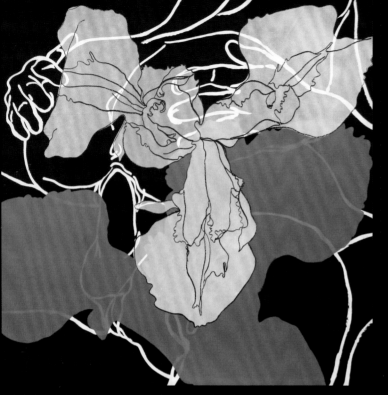

Dirty Flowers 2006
Personal work; drawing, screen print.
Exhibited at Scream Gallery in London.
© Marcus James

'Floral drawings and limited-edition prints
dealing with sexual intrigue and fantasy.'

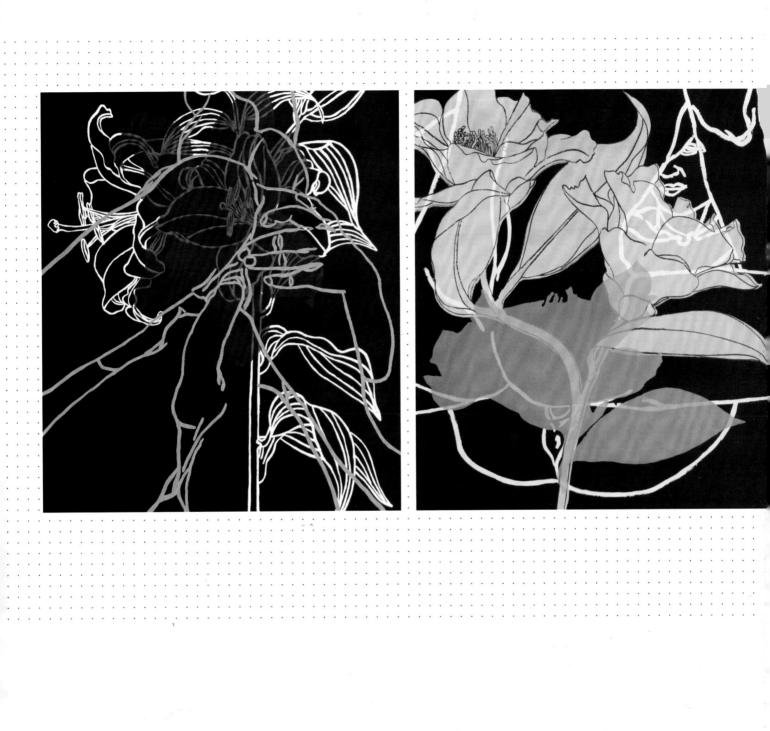

What did you study?
Illustration at Massachusetts College
of Art and Design, Boston.

What inspires you?
Nature and our relationship with it;
television, media and the artificial
sheen of commercials.

What do you collect?
Old magazines and editorials that
constantly inspire my subject matter,
although it's not always apparent.

What is your favourite way of working?
I gather reference material and
ideas, then I lay down the basic
composition, and get going. I love
working on paper; my materials are
pencil, ink, watercolour, plus I like
cutting and painting on wood too.

Where do you work, play and travel?
I work in my home, play in the
mountains and travel to wherever
my eyes will be opened.

Black Raspberry 2008
Personal project; graphite,
watercolour, coffee, paper.
Exhibited at the solo show 'Acid in
the Ice Cream' at Backspace Gallery,
Portland, Oregon.
© Zach Johnsen/Zenvironments

'From a series of large-scale images, this
features a surprise act of violence, a kind
of epiphany or revelation, occurring at a
mundane event, a corporate birthday party.'

X Snow 2008
Client: ESPN Xgames
Apparel design; pen, ink, watercolour, digital.
© Zach Johnsen/Zenvironments

'Series of five images based on extreme
sports (snowboarding, skateboarding,
surfing, BMX biking and motocross), to
be used on apparel and equipment. This
drawing is inspired by snowboarding.'

James Joyce

What did you study?
Graphic Design at Kingston University;
I'm a self-taught illustrator.

What inspires you?
Anything and everything; unusual occurrences
and everyday things in unusual contexts; great
ideas; art.

What do you collect?
Unusual objects, images and postcards.

What is your favourite way of working?
I like to create images based on ideas, by hand,
using a pen, a computer and screen printing.

Where do you work, play and travel?
My studio in east London.

Drawings and Other Objects 2008
Personal project; silkscreen prints,
limited-edition giclée prints, 3D cubes
made of painted birch wood.
Solo exhibition at Kemistry Gallery in London.
© James Joyce

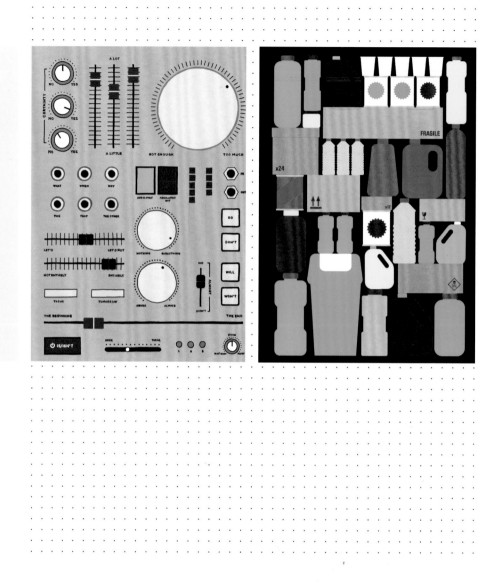

This This This and This 2008
Personal project; limited-edition
giclée print.
© James Joyce

Dials and Dilemmas 2008
Personal project; limited-edition
giclée print.
© James Joyce

Chemical World 2008
Personal project; limited-edition
screen print.
© James Joyce

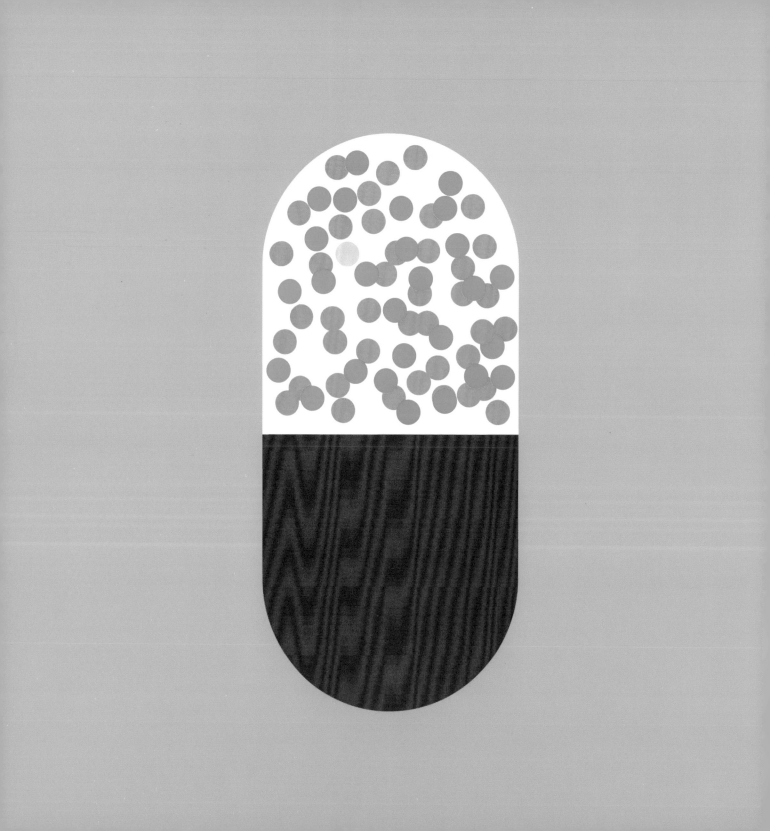

Positive Light 2008
Personal project; limited-edition
giclée print.
© James Joyce

Oh Me Oh My 2008
Personal project; limited-edition
silkscreen print on Colorplan.
© James Joyce

The Guardian Guide 2008
Client: The Guardian Guide
Art director: Stephen Jenkins
Cover illustration.
© James Joyce

Miki Kato

What did you study?
I'm a self-taught illustrator.

What inspires you?
Familiar nature, human relationships.

What do you collect?
Dictionaries about nature (animals, insects, flowers, human biology).

What is your favourite way of working?
I wait until I'm inspired and then draw every little image that I think of, until I've formed a whole image. I draw on cartridge paper with a fine Biro, and I carve into glass with a needle tool. I make images for books, magazines, fashion, advertising and animation.

Where do you work, play and travel?
Work: at home. Play: riversides, bridges.
Travel: anywhere, but it has to be a long vacation.

Face to the Life 2006
Personal project; fine Biro, cartridge paper.
© Miki Kato

'From the series "Woman's Face". Our life shows on our face; what face do you have?'

Real Cat Walk 2007
Personal project; fine Biro, cartridge paper.
Exhibited at Plume Gallery in Paris, and at Lennox Gallery in London.
© Miki Kato

'From the series "Legs". I'm making a connection between nature and humanity.'

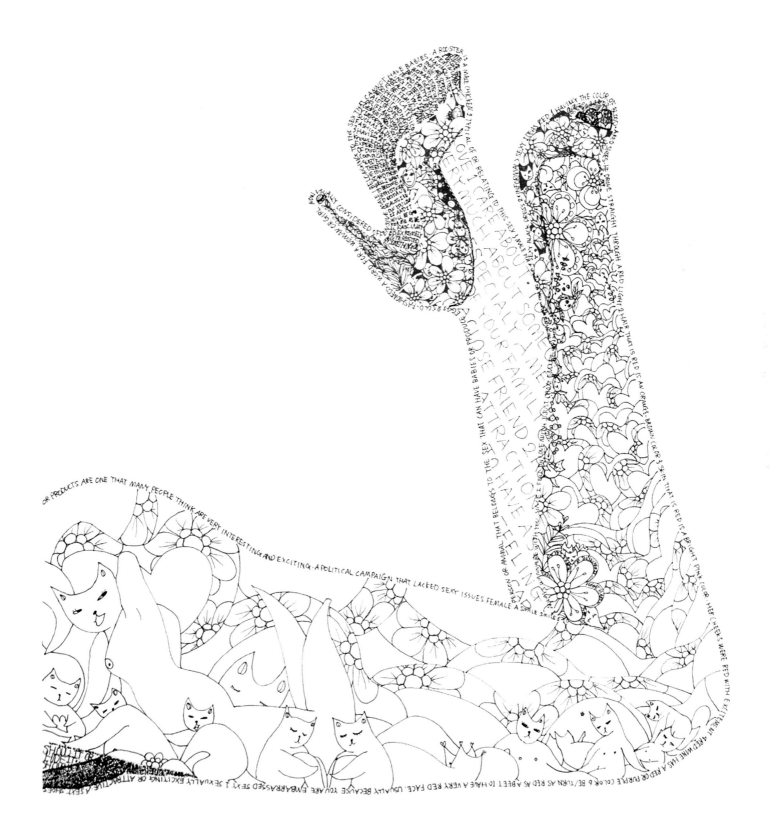

FERNANDO LEAL

What did you study?
Graphic Design in Brazil; Communication Art and Design at Royal College of Art, London. My education in Brazil was mostly technical; I've learned more from working, by trial and error, and exchanging experience and advice with workmates.

What inspires you?
Anything – it's a cliché, but it is true – especially travelling, and discovering unexpected and random elements that you can contemplate with 'foreign' eyes.

What do you collect?
Collage is a major part of my work, so a big pleasure is collecting elements for my image archive; pictures, old book illustrations, drawings, textures. It's important to have a large reference image when you start a job, and even elements that are not used in the final composition may be very inspirational in the process.

What is your favourite way of working?
I don't have a favourite, I like variety and the challenges of different media. But, without any order of preference or hierarchy of process, as it varies from job to job, I use pens, brushes, sketchbooks, graph paper, lightbox, Wacom tablet and Photoshop.

Where do you work, play and travel?
I work at home, but freelancing can be a little isolating, so I like to collaborate, and go places with friends to take photographs that end up in my work.

V.ROM Complexo 12 2004
Client: V.ROM
Calendar illustration; drawings, textures, found images, digitally composed. Exhibited at Resfest in São Paulo.
© Fernando Leal

'The Brazilian streetwear company V.ROM produces a calendar featuring many different image-makers. This illustration is for the month of February.'

Warner Channel 2006
Client: Warner Channel Latin America
Pitch concepts for spot animations; drawings, textures, vector graphics, Photoshop.
© Fernando Leal

'I was invited to art-direct a pitch for the redesign of a television channel; the pitch included spot animations and concept artwork for menus, trigger animations and lower 3rds.'

Untitled 2006
Personal project; drawings, textures,
found images, digitally composed.
© Fernando Leal

'Image created for my website, the
idea being to evoke a surreal and
playful idea of "home".'

Quase 2008
Personal project; still digital
image projected on to installation.
© Fernando Leal

KATHARINA LEUZINGER/MIELO

What did you study?

Graphic Design at Central Saint Martins College of Art and Design, London, but I realized that my real passion was illustration.

What inspires you?

All forms of traditional arts and crafts; patterns of all sorts either random or designed, on any kind of material; naïve painting and art; children's stuff, toys, books.

What do you collect?

Sometimes I think I should collect, as it would de-clutter my brain. Every day I get inspired, and I haven't worked out a clever way of storing all that information, so most of it gets lost before I can write it down.

What is your favourite way of working?

I work straight on to the computer; I just start with a blank canvas (well, monitor screen), and see what happens. The good thing about working on the computer is that I can see several different interpretations of an artwork, which is very useful. I draw in Adobe Illustrator, using a tablet. Sometimes I use Photoshop to add different textures.

Where do you work, play and travel?

I work from London and Paris; work and play are the same thing for me.

Mielo 2007
Personal project; A2-sized promotional poster and cards, ink, paper, Photoshop.
© Katharina Leuzinger

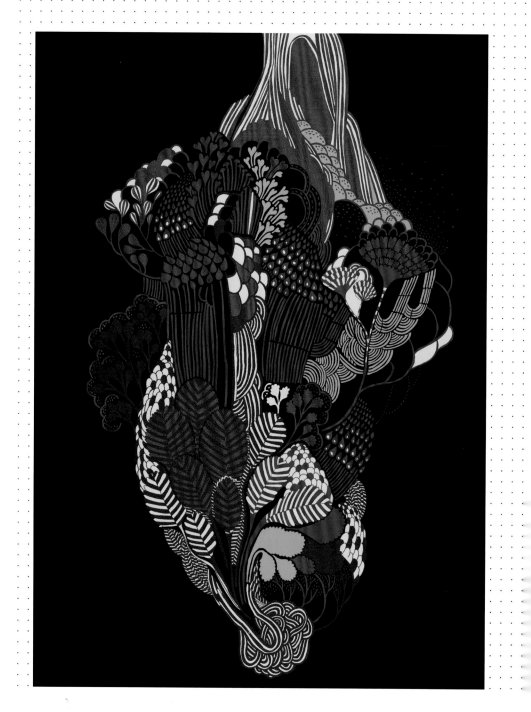

KENZO AMOUR

145

Anne-Pauline Mabire

What did you study?
Graphic Design and Illustration at Olivier
de Serres and La Sorbonne, Paris.

What inspires you?
Nature, feelings, thoughts; I create automatic
drawings from free associations.

What do you collect?
A lot of different things: shells, stones, feathers,
vintage jewellery, little figurines, old postcards
and papers and broken keys.

What is your favourite way of working?
I like to have something in my hand and let it go
on paper; my favourite tools are coloured pencils
and ballpoint pens. Sometimes I put different things
together using a computer.

Where do you work, play and travel?
I'm ready to work anywhere in the world! I'd like
to travel across the Americas (Canada, USA,
South America) on a big road trip some day soon.

Août 2008
Personal project; coloured pencils,
ballpoint pen, computer.
© Anne-Pauline Mabire

'This is a combination of sketchbook
images made during the summer,
which are about nature and love.'

Blossoming 2008
Personal project; pencil, ink, watercolour, paper.
© Anne-Pauline Mabire

'From a series of drawings about smells,
emotions and senses.'

Le Rouget 2007
Personal project; ballpoint pen, gouache, paper.
© Anne-Pauline Mabire

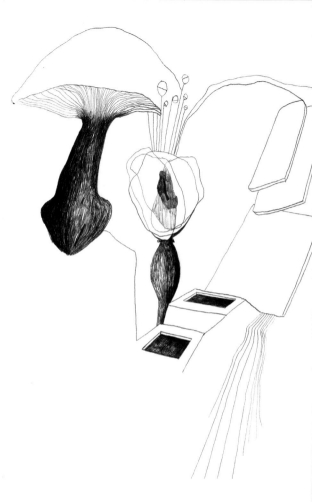

'J'aime Marcher dans les Herbes Hautes' 2007
Client: La Petite Fabrique
Promotional poster; ballpoint pen, old photographs.
© Anne-Pauline Mabire

'This project is for a collective that stages an annual
event and exhibition in a private country garden.
I wanted to express the simple joy of nature.'

Invocation No. 1 2007
Client: La Petite Fabrique
Personal project; coloured pencils,
ballpoint pen, ink, watercolour.
© Anne-Pauline Mabire

'Details of a poster made for the annual
exhibition of "La Petite Fabrique" collective.'

Light Leg 2007
Personal project; coloured pencils,
ballpoint pen, ink, watercolour.
© Anne-Pauline Mabire

'Image from my personal sketchbook.'

Where did you study?
Camberwell College of Arts, but I learnt how to draw from television.

What inspires you?
My first ambition was to drive a tractor.

Where do you work, play and travel?
I work in the great city of London, and I love Norfolk.

Kursk 2008
Personal project; Indian ink on
paper, Photoshop.
Limited-edition print, exhibited at
'Blisters on My Fingers', at MC Motors, Dalston.
© Harry Malt

THE DRAIN I HEARD

SOMEQUESQUEST

MONEY FUN

BLOODY NOSE
LOSS OF SIGHT
BANGING PAIN
ROTTED BRAIN
ANOTHER FUCKING WEEKEND
ARE WE STILL HAVING

MASA

What did you study?
Design; I'm a self-taught illustrator.

What inspires you?
Music, movies, geometric forms, vintage objects from the 1950s to the 1970s.

What do you collect?
Sneakers, vinyl toys, Planet of the Apes memorabilia, Atari video games.

What is your favourite way of working?
I like to research a concept, do initial pencil sketches, then make marker drawings on separate paper layers for each element or colour. Then I scan these, incubate the idea for a day or two, and go back to decide on the final artwork. I'll use Posca markers, drawing pens, scissors, X-Acto knives, the computer, a digital camera and a scanner. I'm currently testing a Cintiq LCD drawing tablet. I'll work in all media, the more difficult the better.

Where do you work, play and travel?
I work at home; it's my studio. I have a big table, music, a computer and the Internet. I play Wii and vintage video games. I travel to Mexico, London, Barcelona, Copenhagen, Tokyo, Los Angeles and Buenos Aires.

Stripe Boy, All Over Girl 2007–8
Personal project; marker pens, Rapidographs, vellum paper, Photoshop.
Published in Novum and a!.
© MASA

'Each line stroke and fill is made on an individual sheet of paper, scanned and composed using the computer. These are self-promotional images, in a series of urban youth portraits, mixing illustration and graphic patterns.'

Logoland 2006–7
Collection of personal and commissioned projects; hand-drawn, vector graphics. Published in <u>Los Logos</u>, <u>Dos Logos</u>, <u>Très Logos</u>
© MASA

'This mix of illustrations and logotypes combined many different projects, from T-shirt designs to corporate identities.'

Hand Made 2008
Personal project; wood blocks.
© MASA

'This is a self-promotional project, aiming
to produce a typeface using basic forms
and keeping a handmade look and feel.'

Guitar Girl 2005
Client: Volkswagen
Fox Hotel Wallpaper mural; markers, collage,
textures, vector graphics.
© MASA

'This mural welcomes guests to the Hotel Fox,
Copenhagen, and is in all the hotel's stairways.'

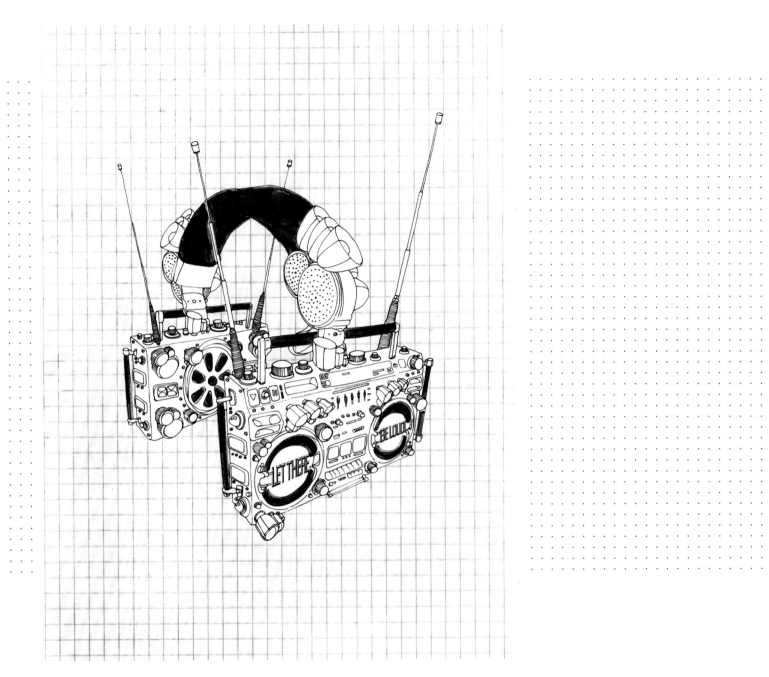

GhettoBlaster 2007
Personal project; marker pens, Rapidographs,
vellum paper, Photoshop.
© MASA

'This was a pitch for a Nokia UK campaign,
and features headphones with bling,
hip-hop attitude.'

Ivan Mayorquin

What did you study?
Graphic Design, and one of the components was illustration.

What inspires you?
My family and my childhood.

What do you collect?
Movies and Futurama memorabilia.

What is your favourite way of working?
Closed eyes, imagining, sketching; I work the digital way, with the computer, and with screen printing; I also want to do some graffiti.

Where do you work, play and travel?
I live and work in Mazatlan, Mexico; London looks like a cool place, and also Spain and Argentina, but if I could, I'd go around the world.

Aevumetria 2008
Client: Aevum Clothing
Series of T-shirt designs;
Adobe Illustrator.
© Ivan Mayorquin, Aevum Clothing

'Aevum featured geometric, clean-cut designs in their first season; so for the next season I decided to go a little more organic and freeform. Nature isn't perfectly geometric and that's what inspired me.'

LOMPIZ 2007
Client: Graficante
Blog header/banner; Adobe Illustrator.
© Ivan Mayorquin, Graficante

'This was for a design collective in Sinaloa, Mexico, that I'm a member of; I tried to do something different – basic, flat figures – to take the blog in a new direction.'

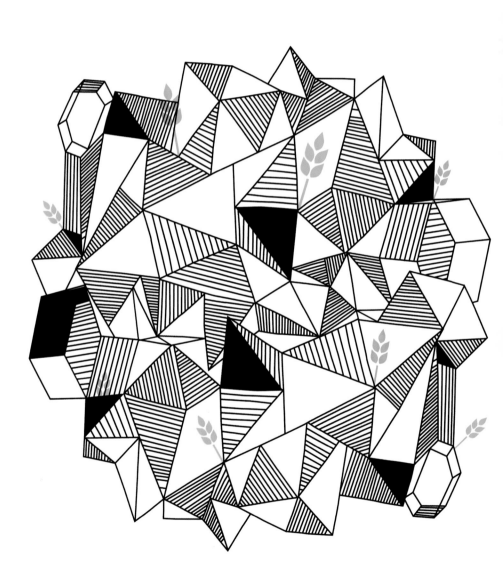

T.O.S. 2008
Personal project; pen and
pencil drawing, Adobe Illustrator.
© Ivan Mayorquin

'From the "Jack Sheridan" series of prints;
this is about freedom, and lost and found
identity; it's about looking inside our heads
and inviting everyone else to see too.'

Meñique 2008
Personal project; digital illustration,
screen print.
© Ivan Mayorquin

'Limited-edition print for the exhibition,
"Blisters on My Fingers", at Print Club
in London. This is about creating, and
the things that come from our fingers.
Sometimes they go in a direction we
didn't plan, and that's good too.'

ÁTILA MEIRELES

What did you study?
I'm a self-taught illustrator.

What inspires you?
Nature.

**What is your favourite way
of working?**
Mixing commercial and experimental
projects, for books, magazines,
websites and more.

Where do you work, play and travel?
Brazil.

Under the Noir 2008
Client: Hell Group
Personal project; A3-sized poster
and online showcase.
© Átila Meireles

'The Hell Group invited me to show my
vision of "noir". I tried to explore and be
playful, showing that noir is in everything
and everyone; it is on land and at the
bottom of the sea, it's alive.'

Notorious 2008
Print illustration; ur
A3-sized poster.
© Átila Meireles

'This is about expla
the surf universe.'

Love and Ipsum 2008
Personal project; type treatment,
vector graphics, A2-sized poster.
© Átila Meireles

'This is about true love; love you,
love all and be free.'

Gabriel Moreno

What did you study?
Fine Art; I'm a self-taught illustrator.

What inspires you?
The human figure, especially the female form; curves, sensuality, eyes, lips, expressions.

What do you collect?
All types of images from magazines, newspapers and photographs.

What is your favourite way of working?
I make images for editorial and advertising, working by hand, using Pilot pens, inks, watercolours and paper, and staying away from the computer until the last, unavoidable moment.

Where do you work, play and travel?
Córdoba, Madrid and New York.

Woody 2008
Client: Neo 2
Editorial illustration; Pilot pen, ink,
newsprint, Wacom tablet, digital.
© Gabriel Moreno

'This composition combines different
images, inside Woody's head.'

Head 2006
Personal project; felt-tip
pens, newsprint.
© Gabriel Moreno

'This composition shows a woman
at different times in her life.'

Eno 2007
Client: Orion Books
Book cover; Pilot pen, ink,
Wacom tablet, digital.
For the authorized biography, <u>On Some
Faraway Beach</u>.
© Gabriel Moreno

'I set out to show different aspects of Brian
Eno, embodied in various layers, created by
using different types of lines and marks.'

KATE MOROSS

What did you study?
Graphic Design at Camberwell College of Art;
I'm a self-taught illustrator.

What inspires you?
Shapes, geometry, science, psychology, economics,
mathematics, paper, stationery, colour wheels,
story tellers, long lunches, early breakfasts.

What do you collect?
Toys, mostly modular, structural building toys,
comics and zines.

What is your favourite way of working?
No hesitation, no pencilling in, just going for
it, with a Sharpie Professional marker on thick
cartridge paper.

Where do you work, play and travel?
London, and part of the year in New York;
I guess you could say I was a real NYLON girl.

YCN Letter 'K' 2007
Client: YCN/Young Creatives Network,
Alex Bec and book team
Book illustration; isometric rendering from
an orthographic drawing of a letter K.
© Kate Moross

'26 different designers and illustrators were
invited to create a letter for the project
BOOK 0708.'

Gossip and Comanechi 2007
Tour poster; hand-drawn,
Wacom tablet, Adobe Illustrator.
© Kate Moross

'I know the band, and they asked
me to design a poster for their tour.
100 were printed and sold at venues.'

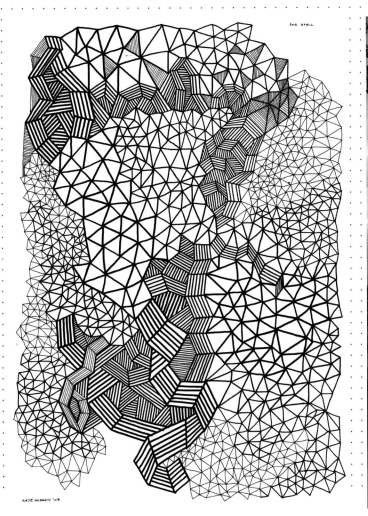

BW55 2007
Personal project; pen on paper.
Exhibited at 55DSL in London.
© Kate Moross

'This A3-sized drawing was made for a friend who worked for
55DSL. I was asked to contribute an image to an exhibition
on the theme "Harmonic Distortion", so I generated a simple
black-and-white pattern, and gave it to my friend after the show.'

Topshop Live Window Doodle 2008
Client: Topshop
Live performance; Posca markers.
© Kate Moross

'3.5 x 3-metre drawing, to launch a capsule collection
at Topshop Oxford Circus. I chose elements from the prints
on the clothing, and drew them over the window, walls and
floor, while interacting with the public and being filmed.'

Don't Panic, War 2007
Client: Don't Panic
Poster; Copic and Pantone markers, card.
© Kate Moross

'Originally I drew this for the War issue of Don't Panic; thousands were printed and it was included in the pack of flyers. Later it was used as a Moo Card, and for a Ford Fiesta advertising campaign.'

Silver-foiled T-shirt 2008
Model: Hans Lo
Personal project; American Apparel T-shirt, foil print.
© Kate Moross

'Limited edition; this is from a series of garments printed
with a labyrinth design; my name is written within the isometric
pattern, but it takes a few minutes of looking to see it.'

Cutting Pink With Knives 2008
Personal project; two-colour screen print.
© Kate Moross

'Limited-edition A2-sized poster. I designed the typography for
this band's record, Populuxxe, on my label, Isomorph Records,
and wanted to work more with the typeface. Pure Groove, the
record shop, invited me to exhibit my work and records at their
new shop launch, so I designed the poster for the exhibition.
With thanks to the band, Cutting Pink With Knives.'

What did you study?
Graphic Design at Willem
de Kooning, Rotterdam;
I'm a self-taught illustrator.

What inspires you?
The freedom of skateboarding
and the idea that Picasso also
started with a white canvas.

What do you collect?
Labels from clothing.

What is your favourite way of working?
I work with good music and a good
vibe, using paper, shears, wood
and Adobe Illustrator.

Where do you work, play and travel?
Amsterdam and Berlin.

Optical 2008
Collaborator: Matt Burvill
Personal project; paper, digital.
Published in Computer Arts.
© Jarrik Muller/Get Busy Fok Lazy,
Matt Burvill

'Working in collaboration, we
challenged ourselves to create
a new typeface in response to a
randomly chosen word, "optical".'

MOUTH

Mouth 2008
Personal project; paper, digital.
© Jarrik Muller/Get Busy Fok Lazy

'A2-sized poster, part of a series that
experiments with type, words and colour.'

What did you study?

Visual Communication at Gobelins l'école de l'image, Paris; I'm a self-taught illustrator.

What inspires you?

Everything is a source of inspiration: architecture, industrial design, fashion and editorial design are my main sources.

What do you collect?

Any flyer, brochure, or beautiful magazine; they're like masterpieces, but I'm running out of space at home.

What is your favourite way of working?

I like to start with a detail or some photographic elements and work out, drawing around them with the computer. I add scanned material, such as dust, paint and ink into the composition, and integrate all the elements in Photoshop. Music, fashion and magazines are my favourite media.

Where do you work, play and travel?

I like to work wherever I am, at night, as long as I'm alone. I love the UK and big cities.

OOK 2008
Personal project; drawing, scanned image, digital composition.
© Pierre Nguyen

'From a series of images conveying personal emotions, focusing on objects, vision, feelings and onomatopoeia.'

Rebrand My City 2008
Client: Computer Arts
Magazine illustration; drawing, photograph, digital composition.
© Pierre Nguyen

'The article was about designing graphic identities for entire cities, so the idea was to show the architectural elements of the city in shapes and lines, straight and curved.'

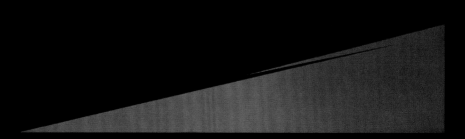

Glance 2008
Client: <u>Volt</u>
Magazine illustration; drawing,
photography, scanned image,
digital composition.
© Pierre Nguyen

'The aim was to convey a personal
perception of the fashion industry, by
way of subtle glimpses of skin, elegant
movement of fabric, exhibitionism
and glances.'

The Curve, Draft 2008
Personal project; drawing, scanned
image, digital composition.
© Pierre Nguyen

Oh Yeah Studio/ Hans Christian Øren and Christina Magnussen

What did you study?
Graphic Design at Westerdals School of Communication, Oslo, and Central Saint Martins College of Art and Design, London.

What inspires you?
Dreams and emotions.

What do you collect?
Everything.

What is your favourite way of working?
We use hand-drawing and Adobe software to make images for print and motion.

Where do you work, play and travel?
The Oh Yeah Studio!

3 uker 2008
Personal project; hand-drawing, vector graphics.
Exhibited at solo show, '3 uker' in Oslo.
© Oh Yeah Studio/Hans Christian Øren and Christina Magnussen

'We printed 200 posters for this exhibition project (entitled "3 weeks" in English), which was based on drawing and abstraction, using both handmade and digital shapes.'

CHRISTINA MAGNUSSEN OG HANS CHRISTIAN ØREN   4 - 24 FEBRUAR 2008   THERESES GATE 5

Beautiful/Decay 2008
Client: Beautiful/Decay
Editorial illustration; hand-drawing, digital.

It Could Be Me, But It is Actually Paul Paper 2008
Client: couldbe.me
Personal project; hand-drawing, digital

I Am a Man 2008
Client: D2
Editorial illustration; hand-drawing, digital.

Whale 2008
Client: Whaleless

SANDRINE PAGNOUX

What did you study?
Graphic Design in Paris; I'm a self-taught illustrator.

What inspires you?
Photography, models, glances; also, films, poetry, music.

What do you collect?
The wall above my computer is covered with a lot
of stuff that inspires me – photographs, drawings,
paintings, words, from Basquiat, Frida Kahlo, Patti Smith,
Marianne Faithfull, Egon Schiele, Tricky, Gainsbourg,
Ian Curtis, Béatrice Dalle, Michael Stipe, Galliano.
I look at them and they support me.

What is your favourite way of working?
The method isn't important; I have lots of methods that
I combine, depending on what I'm searching for. I love
to mix different materials. Working with photography
allows me to use real people, real glances and emotions;
then I incorporate spontaneous elements, drawings,
handwriting, lettering, textures, to recreate my own
vision of these people. My tools are: pen, paper, scissors,
scanner, drawing tablet, computer, Photoshop. I work across
media, including magazines, music and fashion industries,
because each allows me to express myself differently.

Where do you work, play and travel?
I like to work at home, travel to capital cities, or just inside
my head.

Distant Fingers 2008
Personal project; drawing, photography.
© Sandrine Pagnoux

'Life is not very serious; we feel beautiful and
powerful, but inside we're just little clowns, even
our tears are in flashy colours. Life may seem
tragic, but it's really a joke. The title comes from
a song by Patti Smith; I'm a big fan. This image
was used by the fashion label UNDIZ.'

Bestiary 2006
Photographer: Sophie Etchart
Personal project; photography, digital.
© Sandrine Pagnoux

'Series of three, investigating decomposition, based on
the same photography. The idea is to show the transformation
of the human shape, as the man becomes a machine.'

SUNIL PAWAR

Where did you study?
Bath College.

What inspires you?
Good music.

What do you collect?
Old record covers and vintage
sports memorabilia.

**What is your favourite way
of working?**
Freehand drawing, spray-painting on
to wood, layering different textures.

Where do you work, play and travel?
London and New York City.

Premium Street Beats 2007
Personal project; spray paint,
metallic paint, wood.
Exhibited at Flawless & Co. in London.
© Sunil Pawar

'Series of paintings on the subject
of battling DJs.'

Selector Operator 2008
Personal project; spray paint, wood.
Exhibited at Scion Installation in
Los Angeles.
© Sunil Pawar

'This is about the traditional sound
system, and uses terms that are
commonplace in that culture and
environment. As well as being an
artist, I'm a DJ too.'

MIKE PERRY

What did you study?
Graphic Design; I'm a self-taught illustrator.

What inspires you?
Everything.

What do you collect?
Books, pieces of paper, records.

What is your favourite way of working?
Drawing with a pencil.

Where do you work, play and travel?
Work: my studio. Play: Prospect Park.
Travel: Argentina.

Shapes 2008
Personal project; pencil, marker pen.
© Mike Perry

Reloaded 2008
Client: Reloaded
Magazine cover; mixed media.
© Mike Perry

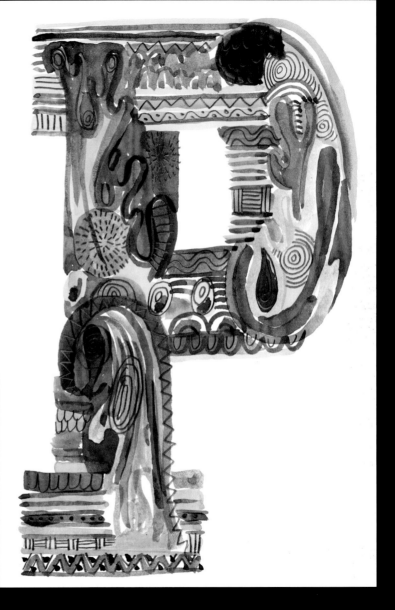

6 Scape 2008
Client: You Work for Them
Limited-edition poster;
three-colour screen print.
© Mike Perry

P 2008
Personal project; pencil, watercolour.
© Mike Perry

What do you collect?

Old magazines, illustrated and art books, pictures I find online and all kinds of flyers and postcards.

What is your favourite way of working?

My approach is quite experimental; I rarely do any sketches before the final piece. I like to work spontaneously and intuitively, without knowing how the final image will look. I work by hand, painting, drawing and collaging, using ink, watercolours and acrylics. Then I compose and retouch the images using a computer.

The Good and the Evil 2006
Personal project; transparent film, frame.
Published in Rojo®mich.
© Karina Petersen

'Series of seven illustrations made using four sheets of transparent film layered with 6mm spaces between each.'

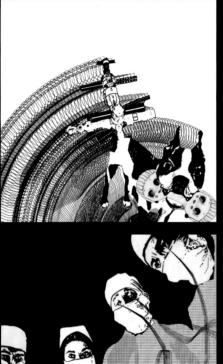
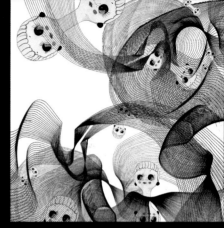

What do you collect?
Old books.

**What is your favourite way
of working?**
I select images that relate to the
concept or the argument, and then
I start to reassemble them, using
a photocopier, cutter and glue.
The final illustrations are used in
advertising and publishing.

Where do you work, play and travel?
I would like to work in the countryside,
play football and visit Japan.

Bolas 2008
Personal project; collage.
© Lorenzo Petrantoni

'A3-sized image using
encyclopaedia images.'

Money 2008
Personal project; collage.
© Lorenzo Petrantoni

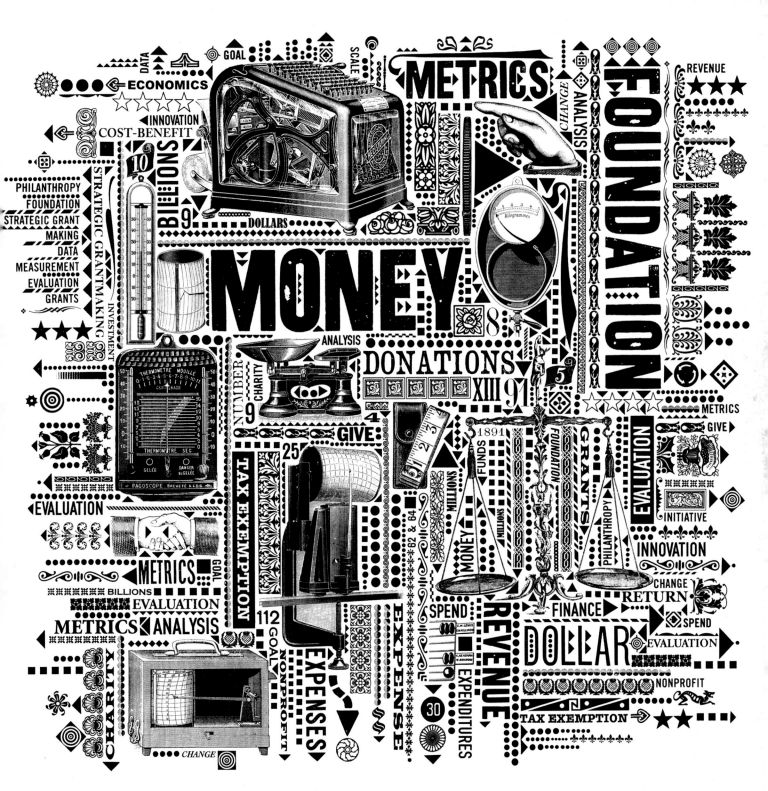

Nike 2005
Client: Nike
Advertising images; collage.
© Lorenzo Petrantoni

'This six-month campaign for China,
featuring the tennis player Maria Sharapova,
included outdoor advertising and
point-of-sale. The images are
based on the concepts "strong like
iron" and "building nice fires".'

ERIN PETSON

What did you study?
Graphic Arts and Illustration at Liverpool John
Moores University.

What inspires you?
Drawing, nature, everyday life; I love patterns and paper.

What do you collect?
Lots of paper, old books, magazines, postcards, fabrics.

What is your favourite way of working?
By hand, drawing in pencil and creating texture with paint,
ink and collage. I use pencil and paintbrush, especially
really thin brushes.

Where do you work, play and travel?
Work: the studio. Play: east London. Travel: Turkey,
to swim and be inspired by the people and by nature.

Tree Women 2007
Personal project, prints and drawings;
pencil, paints, ink, collage, Photoshop.
© Erin Petson

'A series of prints and original drawings for
an exhibition at the Coningsby Gallery
in London, exploring forms and textures.'

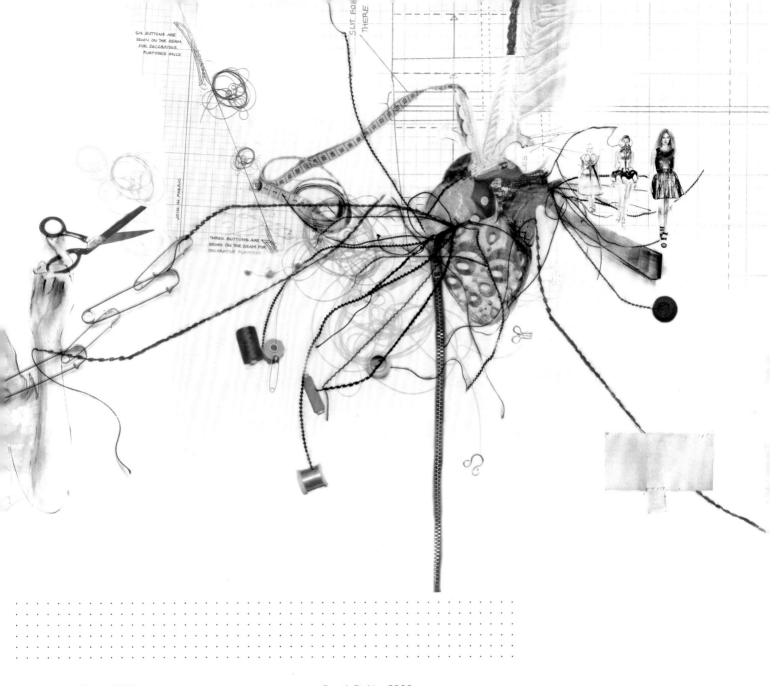

Flora and Fauna 2007
Client: Art Department Publications
Personal promotional work, limited-edition
book; pencil, ink, paint, collage, Photoshop.
© Erin Petson

'This book of illustrations is based on the
themes of fashion illustration and flora
and fauna.'

Breath Fashion 2008
Client: Cheerios USA, Saatchi & Saatchi
Advertising campaign; drawing and collage.
© Erin Petson

'The illustration is based on a human heart,
with fashion running through the veins,
highlighting various fashion elements and
sewing elements.'

QIAN QIAN

What did you study?
Digital Media Design at University of
Edinburgh; I'm a self-taught illustrator.

What inspires you?
Visual arts, music, product design,
fashion, travel, nature.

What do you collect?
Guitars.

What is your favourite way of working?
I always expect the unexpected; I use
a computer to make digital images.

Where do you work, play and travel?
I like to work at home, and I love
going to the beach.

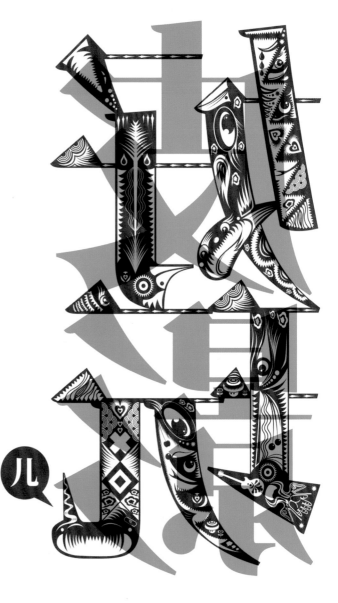

Shadow Play is Fun! 2006
Client: China Shadow

Cows in the Sky 2006
Personal project; Adobe Illustr
© Qian Qian

'This is a one-off A3-sized pri

CORINNA RADCLIFFE

What did you study?
Illustration at the University of Brighton.

What inspires you?
Travelling, my photographs, unusual signs, patterns, colours, Indian art (both traditional and commercial), Victorian decorative design and type, Japanese woodblock printing, 1960s posters.

What do you collect?
Old tins, advertising and toys from the 1950s; books of illustrations and photographs; pattern references from sweet wrappers, envelopes, wallpapers, and natural patterns from woodgrains, flowers and rock formations.

What is your favourite way of working?
I combine hand-rendering and digital techniques, collage and drawing. I begin by hand-sketching rough ideas, then draw elements and scan, colour, add pattern and texture, using Adobe Illustrator and Photoshop. I'd like to work on a larger scale too, doing set design, window displays and limited-edition products.

Where do you work, play and travel?
Work: my spare-bedroom office in Brighton, a short walk from the beach. Travel: I've been inspired in recent years by Morocco, Cuba and Thailand.

Jungle 2007
Personal project; hand-drawing,
Adobe Illustrator, Photoshop.
© Corinna Radcliffe

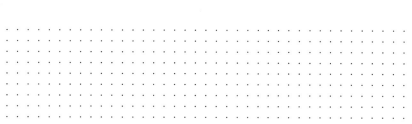

Hansel and Gretel 2007
Personal project; Adobe
Illustrator, Photoshop.
© Corinna Radcliffe

212

Discovering Snoopers Paradise 2008
Client: Lawrence Zeegen, Unmadeup
Book illustration; Adobe Illustrator.
© Corinna Radcliffe

'Each illustrator was asked to describe
a happening unique to Brighton,
for <u>The Brighton Moment</u>, published
during Brighton Festival.'

REVENGE IS SWEET

What did you study?
Graphic Design.

What inspires you?
Life, death, inebriation, dreams, art, music, film,
people and a nice, healthy dose of discontent.

What do you collect?
Anything we can get our hands on; a lot of old
things from secondhand markets and garage sales.

What is your favourite way of working?
Thinking, talking, arguing and agreeing. We love
print in all its forms, but we're up for anything. Screen
printing is a favourite at the moment, but things are
always changing.

Where do you work, play and travel?
We live and work in Hackney, London and spend every
spare moment that we can rushing between our families
and friends in Lyon, France and Melbourne, Australia.

Disconnected Burlesque 2008
Photographer: Mathias Ridde
Personal project; giclée digital prints.
Exhibited at a solo show at Columbia
Road in London.
© Revenge is Sweet

'Series of three, A0-sized, limited-edition
prints. This was a collaboration between us
and our friend, Mathias Ridde; he took the
photographs and we took them apart.'

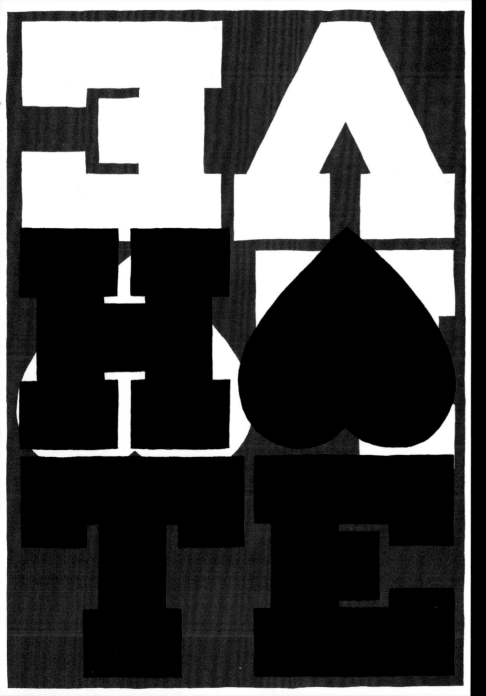

Wild 2008
Personal work; screen print.
Exhibited at "Blisters on my fingers"
at Print Club in London.
© Revenge is Sweet

'Limited-edition, B2-sized print.'

Love & Hate 2008
Personal project; screen print.
Exhibited at a solo show at Columbia
Road in London.
© Revenge is Sweet

'Series of limited-edition, A2-sized prin
based on hand-drawn typography. You
can hang it either way, as hate is love
turned upside down and love is hate
turned upside down.'

Kill Me Softly 2008
Personal project; screen print.
© Revenge is Sweet

'Series of three, A2-sized, limited-edition
prints. These images are inspired by old
Spaghetti Western films. They are to be
used as T-shirt designs by Supersuperficial,
and were exhibited at our solo show, at
Columbia Road in London.'

JANINE REWELL

What did you study?
I'm a self-taught illustrator.

What inspires you?
My life and the world around me are constantly changing, and so are the sources of my inspiration.

What do you collect?
I'm building a picture library of ideas, photographs, designs and colour combinations.

What is your favourite way of working?
I use Adobe Illustrator to make vector-based digital images.

Where do you work, play and travel?
All over the place.

The Beginning of the Word 2007
Client: The Lutheran Congregation of Vantaa
Altarpiece; Adobe Illustrator, hand-painted on to layers of wood.
© Janine Rewell

'This three-dimensional painting is permanently displayed at the Martinristi Chapel. My illustration won a competition for this new altarpiece to be installed in the church's family area, so I kept children in mind when working on the theme and symbols. The illustration tells the story of when the young Jesus started spreading the word of God.'

Dollhouse 2007
Personal project; prints, painted wood.
© Janine Rewell

'This is part of a series of visuals for a doll's house that is
intended to feed a child's imagination, unlike the usual
realistic representation of the interior of a western home.'

KERRY ROPER

What did you study?
Graphic Design and Advertising at
Buckinghamshire College.

What inspires you?
Everything; music, mundane day-to-day life,
offensive images and words.

What do you collect?
Calling cards and old magazines.

What is your favourite way of working?
A total mix, including traditional mark-making,
ink, oil pastels, collage, photography – anything
goes. It's very hands-on; then I compose the
final image digitally.

Where do you work, play and travel?
Work: various. Play: pub. Travel: Cuba.

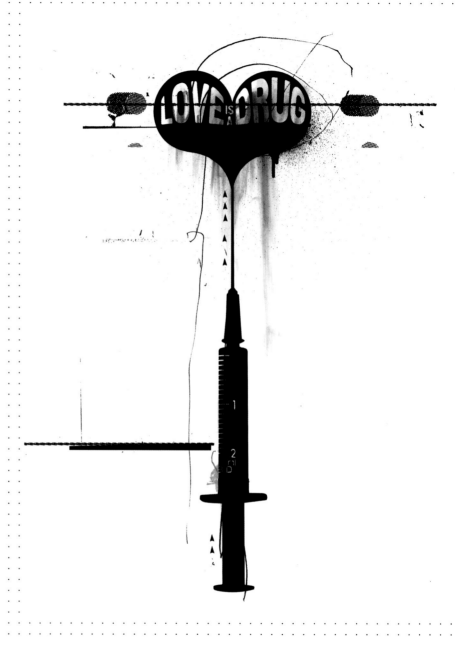

Love is a Drug 2006
Personal project; A2-sized
limited edition, oil pastel, digital.
Exhibited at '4Wall', Fashion Museum
in London.
© Kerry Roper

Time Waits for No Man 2008
Personal project; limited-edition series,
hand-drawn, digital, dye-sublimation on canvas.
Exhibited at solo show 'No Offence Unintended' at the
Conningsby Gallery and at Cosh Soho, both in London.
© Kerry Roper

Dead Souls 2008
Client: Topshop
T-shirt; hand-drawn, digital, screen print.
Also available as a limited-edition canvas,
exhibited at Topshop in London
and Manchester.

Helvetica is Wank 2008
Personal project; limited-edition series,
hand-drawn, digital, dye-sublimation on
canvas.
Exhibited at 'No Offence Unintended'
in London.
© Kerry Roper

CAMILLE ROUSSEAU

What did you study?
3D Animation at Supinfocom, France; Communication Design at Central Saint Martins College of Art and Design, London.

What inspires you?
People, relationships, attitudes, cities, music, textures and classic films.

What do you collect?
Old magazines, from the 1920s to the 1970s.

What is your favourite way of working?
I draw, then scan the images and enlarge details so as to deconstruct the image. I use computers, pencils, old images and glue. I like to work in all media, and am especially interested in moving images; I work with VIEW in Paris, a broadcast design and post-production house, directing and animating.

Where do you work, play and travel?
I like to work with my music; it's my major means of escape. I travel between London and Paris; that's my playground. I'm changing my mind and swapping from one culture to another, as fast as the train moves.

Transition 2007–9 (continues overleaf)
Client: EDF Energy
Illustrations on 25 brown paper bags.
© Camille Rousseau

'What started as a personal project – a reaction to the city of London – came to be used as an advertising campaign by EDF Energy. I used the consumer icon of a carrier bag, which indicates a range of values from everyday to luxury, to reflect scenes of contemporary urban life; the ephemeral object becomes a witness of time and space, and connects people to different locations as they move around the city, carrying and exchanging goods.'

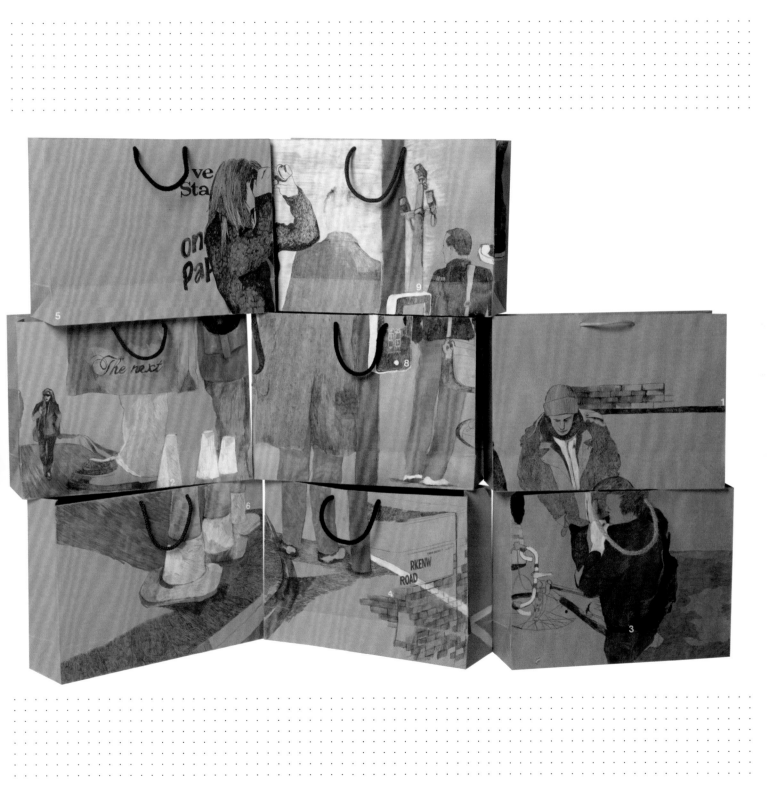

Ryoono

What did you study?
I'm a self-taught illustrator.

What inspires you?
Everything interesting.

**What is your favourite way
of working?**
I draw by hand, and like to work
across all media.

Untitled 2006
Client: Phoenix
Interior design; wall painting.
Installed in the Phoenix Kick
Boxing Gym in Tokyo.
© Ryoono

Untitled 2004
Personal project; wall painting.
Installed at Labline TV in Tokyo.
© Ryoono

Untitled 2008
Personal project; hand-drawing,
pencil, paper.
Exhibited at hpgrp Gallery in Tokyo.
© Ryoono

Danny Sangra

What did you study?
Graphic Design at Central Saint Martins College of Art and Design, London.

What inspires you?
The past, films (mainly bad films), Charles Bukowski, London and the vixens I have met along the way.

What do you collect?
As a kid I collected comics and trading cards. Now, apart from films, nothing. I recently realized that if you collect things, you are using the criteria of what you already like. Instead, why not be inspired by what you never knew existed? So now I am more inspired by randomness.

What is your favourite way of working?
I make a mess first and then deal with it. I use black ink and a fine brush. I produce my best work when I'm bored and not thinking about what I'm doing. I turn on the headphones and put my favourite song of the moment on repeat. I don't like using the same method all the time, but I eventually come back to it, even though I know that I grow tired of things.

Where do you work, play and travel?
In New York I know that I can see friends, hang out and still work. In the summer you can hit the beaches on Long Island, but I need a big city nearby, so I can always work.

Goldielocks Promo 2008
Editor and animator: Fiona Stuart-Bamford for AMS
Music promo.
© Danny Sangra

'I wanted to direct a music video. My friend had a good track, so it started as a personal project as I didn't have to cater to anyone's wishes but mine. I built the set originally for a photoshoot, and my friend suggested I use it for a video, so I adapted the idea. There was no budget, but my producer made a deal with the record company, who funded it in exchange for me painting a mural in their office.'

Alice 2008
Photographer: Chris Brooks
Hair and make-up: Anita Keeling
Model: Alice Rausch
Editorial illustration; hand-drawing,
photography and computer.
© Danny Sangra

'This was originally for a fashion story
but it wasn't used, so I developed it further,
and it was shown in +81 magazine.'

For Luna 2008
Personal project; ink, acrylic paint.
© Danny Sangra

'I was experimenting on paper,
having just finished a commission.
I was in New York, and couldn't bring this
back to London, so I gave it to a friend.'

Coney Wonder Gulls 2008
Personal project; hand-drawing
and photography.
© Danny Sangra

'On Coney Island, I was attacked by massive
seagulls, but you can't help but use the
imagery of the place. This image is part
of a series that functioned as a visual diary.'

and combining technical drawing, watercolours and photography.

Where do you work, play and travel?
I work in my studio, but I like to travel to discover different cultures and styles.

Smoking 2008
Personal project; hand-drawing,
watercolour, digital.
© Martin Satí

'These images are all from a self-promotional publication, Funámbulo, which unfolds into a poster. It is distributed each quarter to creative organizations in Spain.'

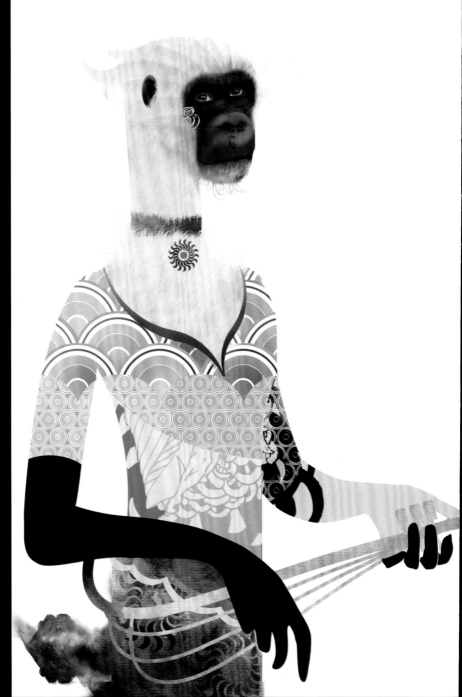

What did you study?
Graphic Design at the School of Visual Arts,
New York City.

What inspires you?
The landscape of Los Angeles, natural forms, vintage
objects, cars, motorcycles, friends and their art.

What do you collect?
Records, skateboards, motorcycles, cards; and
I have a 1950s Seeburg Jukebox.

What is your favourite way of working?
I create pen-and-ink drawings, which I then scan
and manipulate using a computer. I use pen and
ink, spray paint, screen printing and digital media.

Beautiful Losers 2008
Collaborators: Aaron Rose,
Geoff McFetridge (hand-drawn type)
Theatrical film poster; hand-drawing,
pen, photography, Adobe Illustrator.
© Keith Scharwath

Money Mark 2008
Client: Money Mark
Promotional poster; hand-drawing,
pen, Adobe Illustrator.
© Keith Scharwath

'Money Mark is a talented keyboard
player, so I tried to convey that with
my illustration. This poster was used
for Mark's 5x5w showcase.'

Edvard Scott

What did you study?
I'm a self-taught illustrator.

What inspires you?
Everything.

What do you collect?
Experiences and small Japanese
pattern books.

What is your favourite way of working?
I prefer a new method every time;
I use my computer, a sketchpad,
Adobe Illustrator, Photoshop, and
once in a while, After Effects.

Where do you work, play and travel?
Stockholm, and all over the place;
I love going to my family's house in
the Åland archipelago.

Elements: Fire, Metal, Water 2007
Client: K-SWISS
Promotional images for product launch; Adobe Illustrator.
© Edvard Scott/K-SWISS

'The brief from K-SWISS offered a lot of creative scope; each
illustration was to represent a different element (Fire, Water,
Earth, Metal) – one for each shoe in the range – and the visual
language was to communicate the attitude and spirit of K-SWISS.'

Untitled 1, 2 2008
Personal projects; Adobe Illustrator.
© Edvard Scott

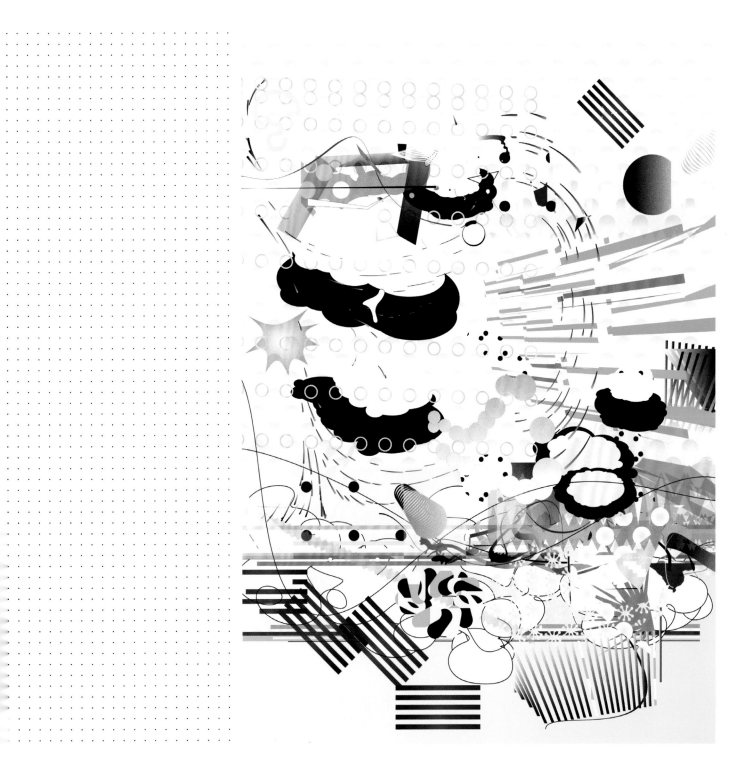

What did you study?
Graphic Design and Advertising
at Buckinghamshire Chilterns
University College.

What inspires you?
It can be anything – music,
movies, television, books. I seem
to find inspiration from many places.

What do you collect?
Music and books.

What is your favourite way of working?
Pen and ink mostly, sometimes
just pencil.

Where do you work, play and travel?
Work: Manchester. Play: gigs.
Travel: New York.

Number 13 Baby 2007
Personal project; pen on paper.
© Si Scott

'Series of images created for solo
exhibition, "Ink and Lyrics", in London
and Chicago.'

100% Design Tokyo 2006
Client: Designers Block
Posters; pen and paper,
screen printed in fluorescent ink
on ply and board.
© Si Scott

'This series of posters on the
theme of love was exhibited at
Designers Block in Tokyo.'

ℰℛesonate

PIGEON

By Si Scott
for Silvan Records 2007

www.silvanrecords.co.uk
www.silvanonline.co.uk

ℰℛesonate

RAM

By Si Scott
for Silvan Records 2007

www.silvanrecords.co.uk
www.silvanonline.co.uk

Resonate 2008
Client: Silent Studios
Posters and packaging; pen and paper.
Exhibited at Beyond the Valley in London,

THE HEART OF DESIGN STILL BEATS

Claire Scully

What did you study?

Graphic and Media Design at London College of Communication; Communication Design at Central Saint Martins College of Art and Design, London.

What inspires you?

In the 'real world', nature and the urban environment, but in the 'fantasy world', science-fiction films and books, and anything that seems ridiculously impossible.

What do you collect?

I pick up leaves, pinecones and interesting bits of wood. And I have a growing collection of sci-fi films and ephemera.

What is your favourite way of working?

My favourite tool is my camera; all of my work starts with a photograph and I like to use images that I've taken myself. I mix those photographs with drawing, using the computer. When I get the chance, I like to experiment with other media, to keep things fresh, and will move into staging exhibitions, moving image, 3D and furniture design.

Where do you work, play and travel?

Work: home studio, with everything at my fingertips. Play: in the woods; I like to get my feet on earthy ground and for my eyes to see some green. Travel: mountains and forests and finding new places in the UK that I haven't seen before.

Tower Block Tit, from The Quiet Revolution 2006
Personal project; series of various sized images and a three-minute movie.
© Claire Scully

'I developed a process using the computer because I wanted to screen print but never had enough time. I try to keep the feel organic, and have accepted the process for its own properties and not simply as an alternative option. It allows more freedom to be creative as I can introduce photographic elements more easily than if I was screen printing.'

Itsumaden and the Last City 2008
Personal project; series of various-
sized images, photography, drawing
and digital design.
© Claire Scully

'This change of content and direction
is inspired by my love of science-
fiction films. This project plays with the
concept of time travel and is based on
the idea that there are multiple realities
and alternate universes.'

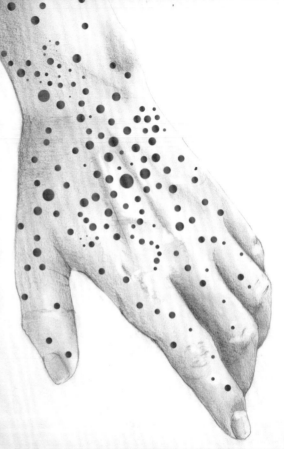

The Quiet Revolution 2006
Personal project; series of various-sized
images and a three-minute movie.
© Claire Scully

New York Times 2008
Client: New York Times
Newspaper illustration in Science
and Nature section; pen, pencil,
digitally applied colour.
© Claire Scully

'This illustration was for an article
about skin irritations.'

Natsko Seki

What did you study?
Illustration at the University of Brighton.

What inspires you?
Antique objects, old books and papers, architecture, architectural models and drawings.

What do you collect?
Little figurines, including toys, dolls and figures from architectural models, plus old postcards, music manuscripts and magazines.

What is your favourite way of working?
I use a Pentel Graph 1000 for Pro mechanical pencil, tracing papers and a Wacom tablet to make collages; my favourite medium is the poster.

Where do you work, play and travel?
I like to work in London; I love brick houses, galleries, museums, shops and pubs. I like to play in Tokyo; I'm always really busy there visiting new galleries and shops, friends and family. It's amazing to see new products, objects and sweets in the supermarkets every time I go back. I like to travel in Scandinavia; the flea markets are full of exciting and colourful objects and the natural environment is great, especially in Finland.

Olde Tyme Circus: Aerial Ballet 2008
Personal project; pencil, papers, found images, old magazines, photography, Photoshop.
Exhibited in 'Retro Perspective' at Gallery ROCKET in Tokyo.
© Natsko Seki

'I like circuses, and I created a series of limited-edition imaginary circus posters, inspired by the aesthetic of antique posters.'

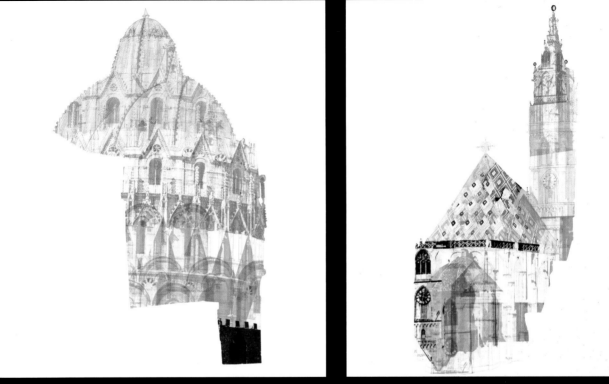

Italy 2008
Personal project; pencil, papers,
found images, old magazines,
photography, Photoshop.
Exhibited in 'Retro Perspective'
at Gallery ROCKET in Tokyo.
© Natsko Seki

For these limited-edition prints,
I created a dynamic cityscape by
collaging beautiful historic buildings
from different Italian cities into one
big image.'

JOHN SLADE

What did you study?
Graphic Design; I was brought up in a
creative environment.

What inspires you?
Abstract forms, daily life, friends, public transport,
toy shops, music...inspiration is a strange beast,
it can come from anywhere.

What do you collect?
Pens and markers, sticker dots, old toys.

What is your favourite way of working?
My approaches consistently contradict themselves;
sometimes it's a mess, sometimes it's clinical.
I use pencils and pens, ink, paints, sticker dots,
screen printing, Adobe Illustrator, Photoshop
and whatever is at arm's reach.

Where do you work, play and travel?
I like to work in an east London studio, with
my friends.

Futile Considerations 2008
Client: Dustin Hostetler/UPSO
Personal project; ink, pen, Photoshop.
© John Slade

'Published in Faesthetic, a print design
project, on the theme of Doomsday,
which I was eager to show as a futile
concept, the idea being that the beginning
and the end of the planet are the same
thing, hence the butterfly paintings.'

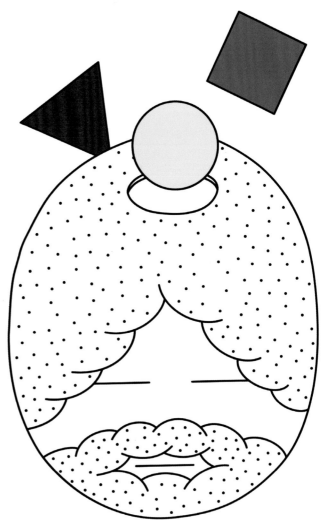

Think About Design 2008
Client: Concrete Hermit
Collaborator: Chris Knight/
Concrete Hermit
T-shirt design; screen printing.
© John Slade

'This simple design evolved from
the pile of drawings I tend to create
on a daily basis.'

Any Block You Dip 2007
Collaborator: Si Scott
Personal project; A1-sized giclée print,
hand-drawing, Adobe Illustrator.
© John Slade

'Exhibited at "Ink and Lyrics" in London,
as part of a show of invited collaborators
illustrating lyrics to various songs. This one,
by Digable Planets, started with a map of
Brooklyn, where the musicians live, and
includes characters for each band member.
Si then added the typography.'

Shadow, Creep 2007
Collaborators: Get Involved, Build
Series of five posters; Adobe Illustrator.
© John Slade

'Two exhibitions were opening on the same
night, with the design group, Build, involved
in each, so they created a canvas coupling
the two nights into one question. The answers
were provided by various illustrators.'

Rose Stallard

What did you study?

Fine Art Printmaking at Norwich School
of Art and Design.

What inspires you?

Youth culture, 1960s and 1970s rock, fanzines,
photography and lo-fi art.

What do you collect?

Photos, rock music and memorabilia, old skate stuff,
underground press publications, fanzines.

What is your favourite way of working?

I draw by hand and then work on my Mac, mixing up my
own drawings with found images from all kinds of sources.
I try and capture the spontaneity and enthusiasm of a
zine, while remaining discerning and professional. I like to
draw freehand and generate images using a computer.
I also screen print, and create surface designs and
print tees. My process includes pen, lightbox, scanner,
computer, screen print.

Where do you work, play and travel?

Work: at my studio. Play: Print Club. Travel: anywhere hot.

My Favourite Stations 2008
Personal project; Wacom pad, computer.
© Rose Stallard

'Series of four prints about my favourite
Internet radio stations.'

Big Noise 2005
Client: Graniph
Personal project; hand-drawn, scanned,
screen print.
Limited-edition T-shirt print.
© Rose Stallard

'This is about making DIY mix-tapes
and rocking out at 2am!'

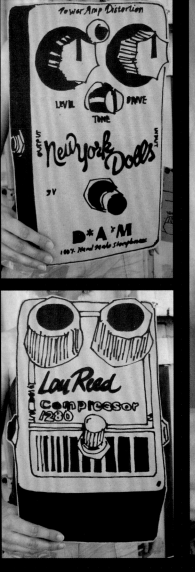

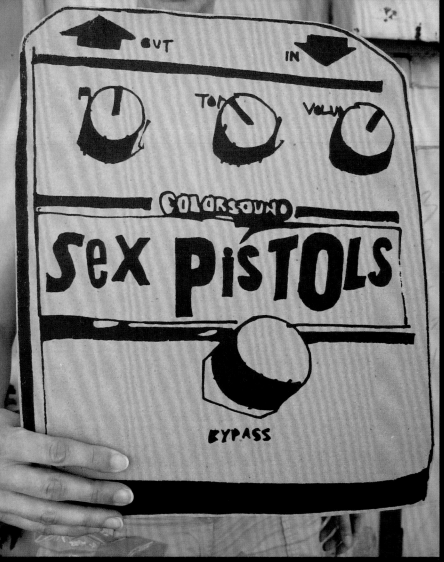

Guitar Pedals 2007
Personal project; hand-drawn, Photoshop,
screen print, cardboard.
Shown at a solo exhibition at Dazed Gallery
in London.
© Rose Stallard

Limited edition, A3-sized. This set of giant,

Badge Wallpaper 2007
Personal project; hand-drawn, Photoshop,
screen printed, lining paper.
Shown at a solo exhibition at Dazed Gallery
in London.
© Rose Stallard

'Covered in drawings of logos and rock badges.'

Rock America 2007
Client: NYLON
Magazine illustration; hand-drawn, digitally coloured.
© Rose Stallard

'The brief was to show the best and most unexpected
music scenes across America, for an issue themed
"Rock America".'

JIM IS
ON FIRE

ELVIS
IS DEAD

LOU IS
WILD

JOHNNY IS
ROTTEN

LEMMY
LIKES GIRLS

KEITH IS
STONED

DONOVAN
IS MELLOW

MARC
IS GLAM

OZZY IS
MY IDOL

Rock Dudes 2007
Personal project; hand-drawn,
Photoshop, screen print.
Limited-edition prints exhibited
at Rough Trade East
in London.
© Rose Stallard

What did you study?
Graphic Design at the
AKV|St. Joost, Breda.

What inspires you?
All kinds of things.

What do you collect?
Lots and lots of books.

**What is your favourite way
of working?**
Concept, sketching, final
development using Adobe Illustrator.

Where do you work, play and travel?
Berlin, Barcelona, London,
Paris, Amsterdam.

Mupi 2008
Personal project; print, Adobe Illustrator.
© Staynice

'This is a graphic self-portrait and was
exhibited at the Graphic Design Festival
in Breda.'

They Come To Feed On Us 2008
Personal project; print,
paper, glue.
© Staynice

'An example of free-expression.'

Playgrounds 2008
Collaborators: The Blouses,
LouLou, Tummie, Zeptonn
Personal project; paint, wood.
© Staynice

'This collaborative project was exhibited
at the Playgrounds Festival in Tilburg.'

Ian Stevenson

What did you study?
Graphic Design at Camberwell College of Art, and a few years after leaving, I started drawing.

What inspires you?
There are ideas everywhere, and when I least expect it, one appears in my head.

What do you collect?
I gather books and strange objects from charity shops, and watch TV.

What is your favourite way of working?
Holding a pen in my hand and drawing on something; when I draw on a real object I only have one go at it, and can't make a mistake. I enjoy thinking of an idea and drawing it with a pen.

Hove Festival 2007
Client: Neighbour
Poster for Hove Festival in Norway.
© Ian Stevenson

'The brief was to create a world of drawing for this new music festival; I drew all the elements separately so that the characters could be used across the entire festival graphics, for websites, programmes, merchandise and print and TV promotions.'

Ruis 2008
Client: RUIS
Magazine cover illustration; pen on paper.
© Ian Stevenson

Rubbish Art 2005–ongoing
Personal project; series of drawings
made directly on to found objects.
© Ian Stevenson

'This project involves walking the streets,
and drawing on to rubbish; it brings the
rubbish to life and makes it talk back.'

Cheeky Bastards 2008
Personal project; limited-edition
giclée print.
© Ian Stevenson

'This was created for my exhibition "Have
a Nice Day" at the Iguapop Gallery in
Barcelona. It featured objects talking
back about how they have been treated.'

Sandra Suy

What did you study?
Fashion Design; I'm a self-taught illustrator.

What inspires you?
Beauty and the immediate pleasure that it provides when you contemplate it; the extravagance of fashion; magazines, photography and films.

What is your favourite way of working?
I will search a concept in Google, collect photographic references and make a collage of ideas. Then I use pencil, paper, a computer and drawing tablet.

Where do you work, play and travel?
Work: my studio. Play: anywhere. Travel: anywhere.

Pucci 2008
Client: So Chic
Magazine illustration; computer.
© Sandra Suy

'Showcasing Pucci's Autumn/
Winter 2008 Collection.'

Toko/Eva Dijkstra and Michael Lugmayr

What did you study?
Graphic Design at AKV|St. Joost, Breda, the Netherlands.

What inspires you?
Art, music, books, nature, architecture, design.

What do you collect?
We stopped collecting things, as the house became too small; now we collect memories.

What is your favourite way of working?
Experimenting and pushing the software on our favourite tool, the Apple Mac.

Where do you work, play and travel?
Everywhere there's power.

State of Mind 2007
Personal project; digital.
© Toko/Eva Dijkstra and Michael Lugmayr

'We created this limited-edition print so as to promote our passion for experimentation, with no brief and no boundaries.'

Code 2005
Client: Code
Magazine illustration; digital.
© Toko/Eva Dijkstra and Michael Lugmayr

'Over a number of years, and since its very first issue, we've created type-image headlines for this street-inspired fashion magazine.'

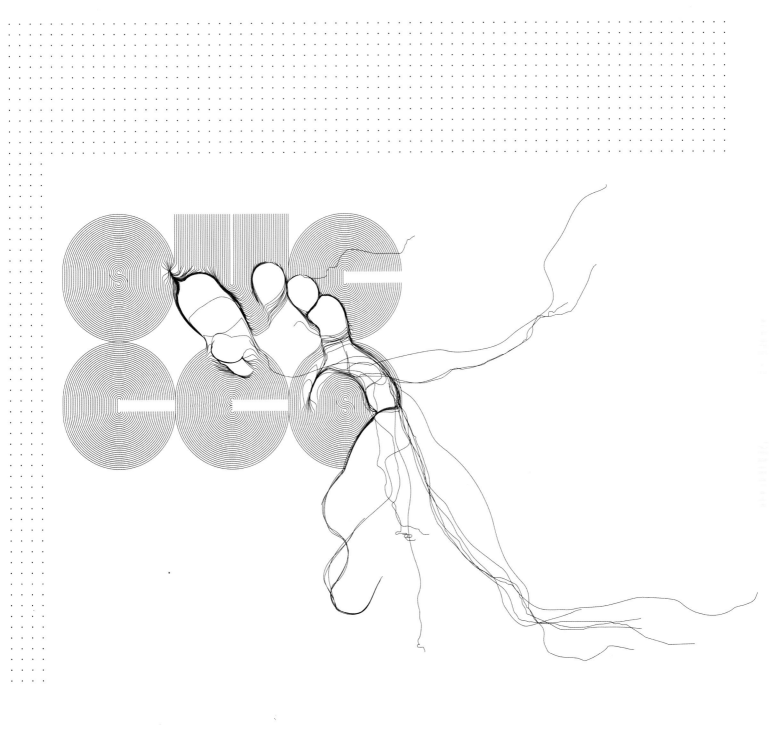

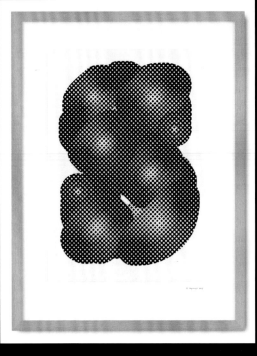

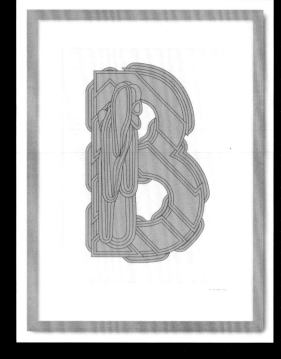

Confused Type 2007
Personal project; screen print.
© Toko/Eva Dijkstra and
Michael Lugmayr

'Limited-edition prints
exploring the visual
and decorative potential
of type forms.'

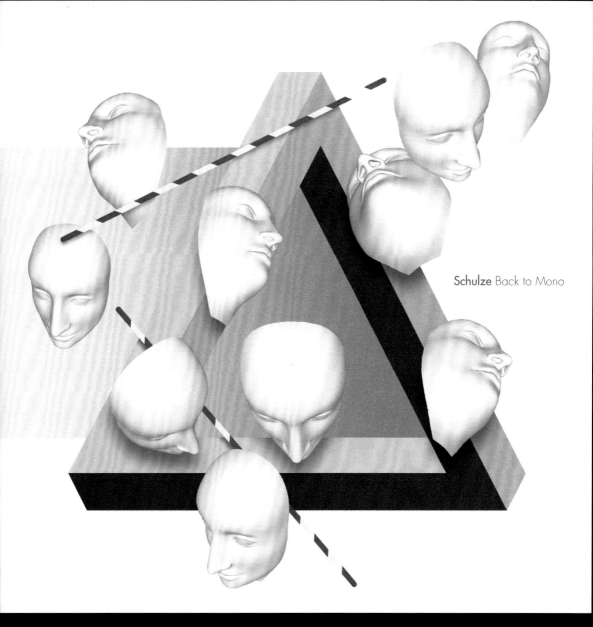

Schulze Back to Mono

ONcovered 2008
Client: Ontwerpatelier
Album cover; digital.
© Toko/Eva Dijkstra and Michael Lugmayr

Inspired by the cheesy album covers of
Klaus Schulze, an early electronic musician,
we created a sleeve design for this "sound

What inspires you?
Nature, design classics, the
Internet and friends.

What do you collect?
Old vinyl records and stamps.

What is your favourite way of working?
I make vector illustrations, calligraphy,
three-dimensional design and
motion graphics.

Where do you work, play and travel?
My ideal would be a desert island
with the Internet.

50 Things We Love 2009
Client: <u>Disappear Here</u>
Magazine cover; digital.
© Alex Trochut

'The headline is represented by a single
image made of letters, a face and a heart'

Clown Monogram 2009
Personal project; digital.
© Alex Trochut

'This personal monogram, using the letters
"A" and "T" from my name, is realized using
Victorian, circus-style lettering.'

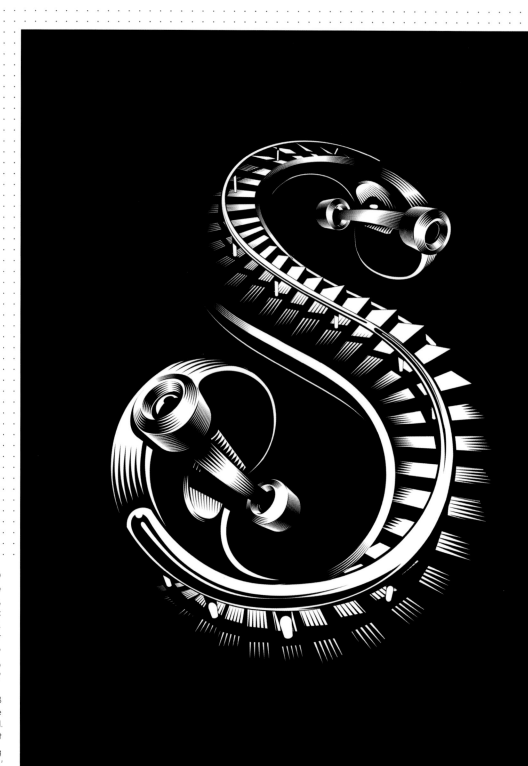

Skateboard 'S' 2009
Client: Converse
Art directors: Anamoly/Ian Toombs,
Mike Byrne, Natalie Bertaux
Advertising image; digital.
© Alex Trochut

'The brief asked that the letter "S"
represent street skateboarding, so
I made it out of a stair rail and a board.'

Music Love, Zune Originals 2008
Client: Zune
Promotional image; laser on metal, digital.
© Alex Trochut

'This is a personal interpretation of a song
for the digital music download site.'

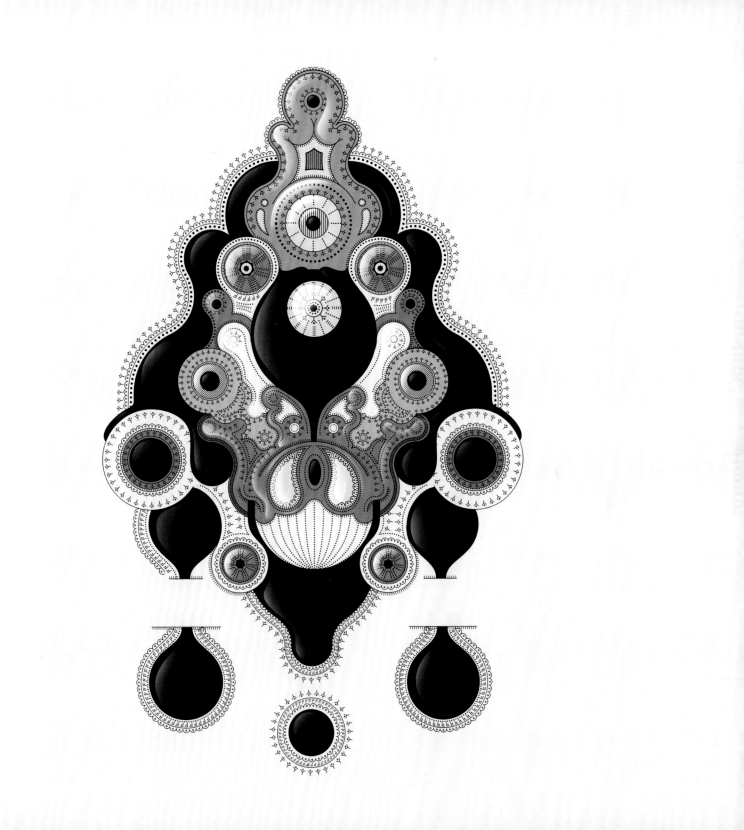

UFEX

Where did you study?
The Danish Design School and Central Saint Martins College of Art and Design, London.

What inspires you?
Shapes.

What do you collect?
Book, books and more books.

What is your favourite way of working?
Constructing and building sculpture and installations; using Adobe Illustrator and Photoshop; drinking tea.

Where do you work, play and travel?
Asia; the rest of the world doesn't matter...

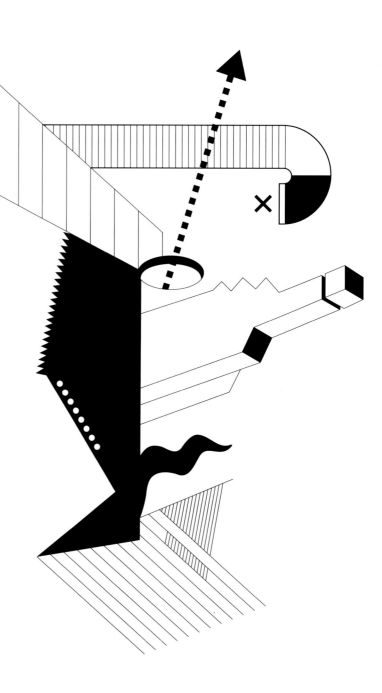

Old Feelings 2006
Personal project; Adobe Illustrator.
© UFEX

'This is an experiment using simple, geometric shapes.'

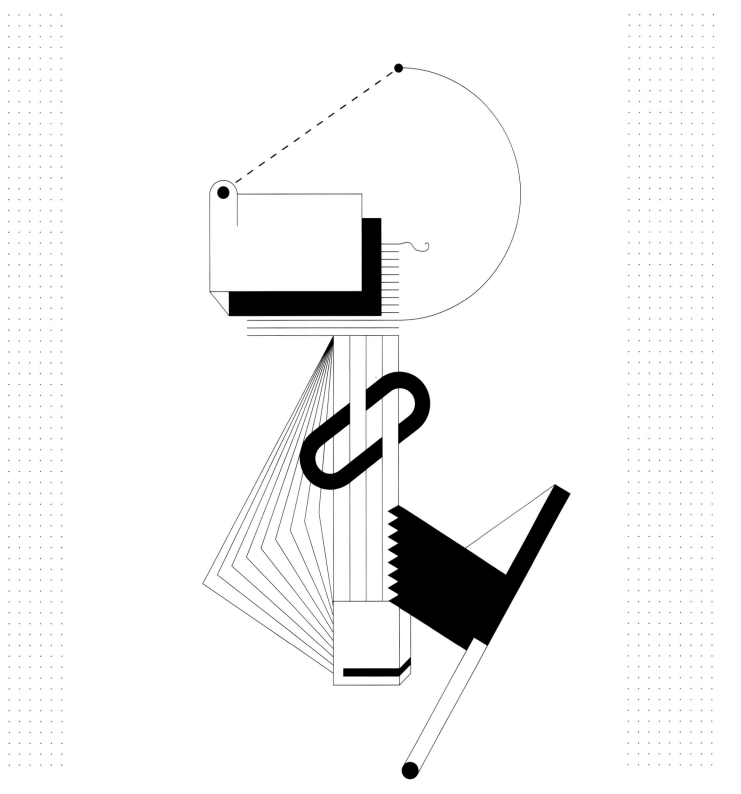

Monster, Mossman 2006
Personal project; promotional posters,
Adobe Illustrator.
© UFEX

and Design, Helsinki.

What inspires you?
My son, weirdness, paganism, religious images, monsters and villains, science, animals, nature, space, music, patterns from around the world, embroidery.

What do you collect?
Books, magazines, images from the Internet, weird-looking objects, records.

What is your favourite way of working?
Imagination, paper cutting, collage, ink, Wacom tablet, Adobe Illustrator, Photoshop; print is my medium.

Where do you work, play and travel?
My home, my studio, my summer place in the countryside, Helsinki, Tokyo. I'd like to visit new places, such as Africa and South America.

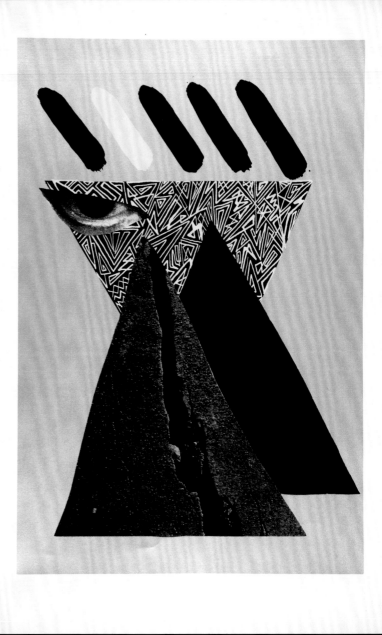

Escalator Xmas Box 2007
Client: Escalator Records
Promotional prints; paper cutting, computer.
© Antti Uotila

'Tokyo-based label Escalator Records asked me to design a set of prints for their Xmas Box, a printed gift bag containing a CD, a cookie, a T-shirt, hoodie and furoshiki (scarf/handkerchief). I designed all the printed textiles.'

WAD 2007
Client: WAD
Magazine illustration; mixed media.
© Antti Uotila

'Every issue, this French pop-culture magazine features fashions from new clothing labels, and a different illustrator designs the spread. This is my version.'

Von/HelloVon

What did you study?
Illustration and Animation at
Kingston University.

What inspires you?
Way too many things to list.

What do you collect?
Records, old Penguin and
Pelican books.

What is your favourite way of working?
80% analogue, 20% digital; a healthy
mixture of pencil, brush, ink, paper
and Mac.

Where do you work, play and travel?
Work: the studio. Play: The
Commercial Tavern. Travel: New York.

All is Full of Love 2007
Personal project; pencil, graphite, ink.
© Von/HelloVon

'Limited-edition, A2-sized and A3-sized
prints, featuring hand-drawn typography.'

Land 3 2007
Personal project; pencil, graphite,
ink, mixed media.
© Von/HelloVon

'Limited-edition, A1-sized print,
exploring a combination of portraiture
and landscape, for a solo exhibition at
Espeis Gallery in Williamsburg, New York.'

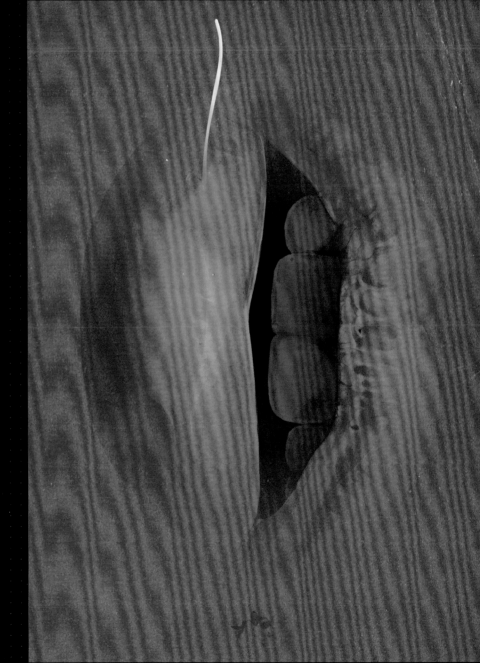

Lascivious 2008
Client: Lascivious
Promotional image; ink, digital.
© Von/HelloVon

'Limited-edition set of playing cards
with custom-designed illustrations
exploring the theme "lascivious".'

SVSV 1, 9 2007
Client: Serum versus Venom
Advertising images; pencil, graphite,
ink, photography, digital.
© Von/HelloVon

Series of ten illustrations for a fashion
collection that create a unique visual
language and atmosphere, without
obscuring the clothes.'

Beetle Shears, Bird Shears 2007
Client: Serum versus Venom
Personal project; pencil, graphite,
ink, digital.
© Von/HelloVon

Original drawings from a series of
three, marrying an animal and an
object. Exhibited at a solo show at
Espeis Gallery in Williamsburg,
New York.'

Lion 1 2007
Personal project; pencil, graphite,
ink, digital.
© Von/HelloVon

'An extension of the Animal series,
this A1-sized drawing explores the
essence and anatomy of the lion.
Published in the Creative Review
Monograph series.'

Ben Walker/benUFO

What did you study?

Fine Art and Graphic Design at Northumbria University;
I'm a self-taught illustrator.

What inspires you?

Song lyrics, album covers and bands from the 1960s and
1970s, such as The Incredible String Band; also children's
illustrator Arthur Rackham and artists Martin Sharp,
Michael English and Boris Vallejo.

What do you collect?

Vinyl from the late 1960s, books, movies, old photographs
and musical instruments.

What is your favourite way of working?

I start working in pencil and sketch in the figures, form
and shape. When I'm happy with the proportions I put
down the ink, watercolour or oil paint, scan and add colour
using layers and blends in Photoshop. Sometimes I live-
trace the scan and add colour using Adobe Illustrator.

Where do you work, play and travel?

Mainly in pubs and cafés around London, in Shoreditch,
Greenwich and Soho. I also spend time on the west
coast of Scotland.

The Sensual Laboratory 2008
Client: <u>Dazed & Confused</u>
Magazine illustration; hand-drawn,
pencils, Fineliner, computer.
© Ben Walker/benUFO

'For a feature about Albert Hoffman, who
discovered the LSD formula, I produced a
non-typical piece – no hippies, flowers or
Yellow Submarines. I wanted to portray the
well-documented darker side of LSD;
the bad trips and the hallucinogenic
feelings that occur with the drug.'

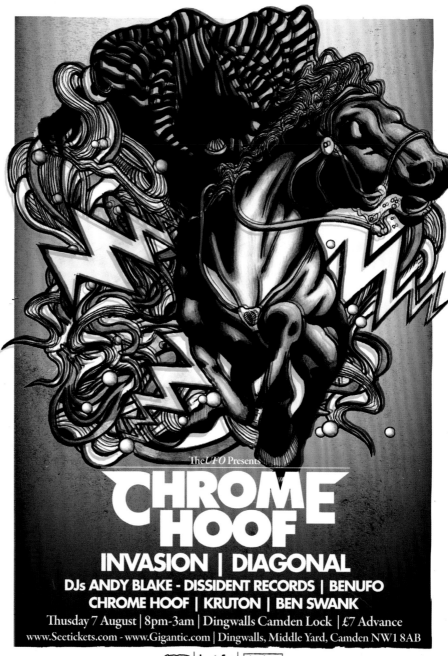

Chrome Hoof 2008
Personal project; hand-drawn,
pencils, Fineliner, computer.
© Ben Walker/benUFO

'This image was used as a
poster for a gig I promoted, with
Chrome Hoof and other bands.
The image reflected the bands'
names, and I wanted to include
a horse and a wizard.'

Don't Panic 2008
Client: Don't Panic Media, 3 Mobile.
Advertising image; hand-drawn,
pencils, Fineliner, Photoshop.
© Ben Walker/benUFO

'Limited-edition A2-sized posters were
distributed free accompanied by a live-
illustration event. This image is intended
to demonstrate the freedom offered by
3 Mobile's Dongle device, which allows the
user to access the Internet from anywhere,
using a USB connector. I tried to convey
the massive amount of information
available to individuals via the Internet,
and used retro-1970s, space-age type
to show how technology has moved on.
The lightning bolts represent the speedy
connection; the waves are the information.'

at Asheville; I'm a self-taught illustrator.

What inspires you?
Life, pop culture, music, art.

What do you collect?
Pictures of broken signs at mini-malls.

What is your favourite way of working?
It all depends on what I want the end result to be; I produce collage, print design, photography and video, using Adobe Illustrator, Photoshop and InDesign.

Where do you work, play and travel?
The Outer Banks, North Carolina.

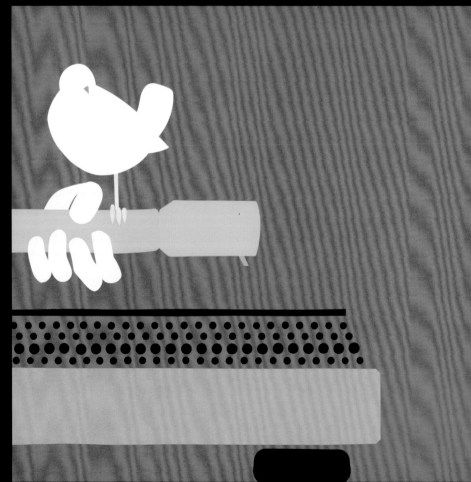

Broken Fader 2007
Client: Broken Fader
Promotional image;
scanned images, Photoshop
© Jarrett Webb/Obsolete Suite

'Some friends in a band asked me for some images for their upcoming release; this complex image reflects the sound of the band.

Hoodstock 2005
Personal project; Adobe Illustrator.
Exhibited at 'Audible Visible' and 'Audible Visible 2' in Winston-Salem and Chapel Hill, North Carolina.
© Jarrett Webb/Obsolete Suite

'This image is about "hippie culture versus DJ culture."'

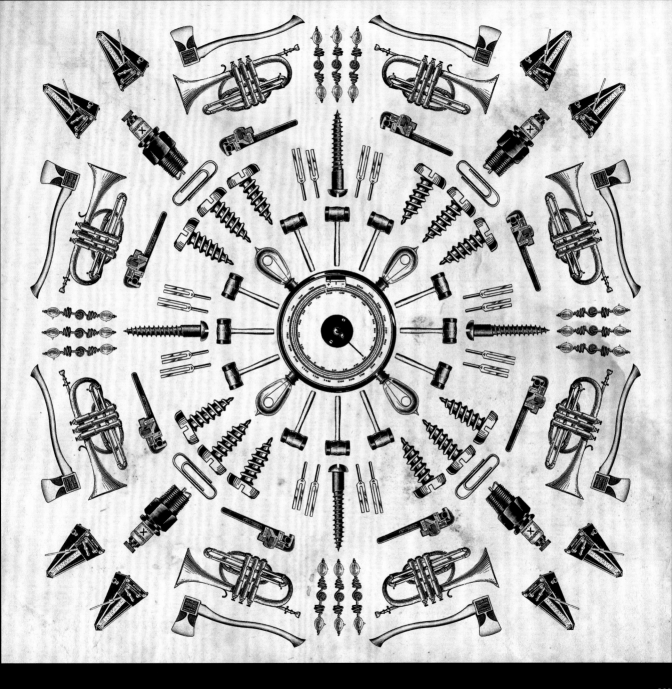

JESS WILSON

What did you study?
Graphic Design and Illustration.

What inspires you?
I enjoy observing the world around me and documenting all sorts of eccentric occurrences.

What do you collect?
Every year I go through my room, rounding up all the bits of pleasing graphics I've collected, stuff like sweet wrappers and cards.

What is your favourite way of working?
First, I draw an image in pencil, then I use a lightbox to add colour and give the image more style. I use pencils, crayons, paints, paper.

Where do you work, play and travel?
I'm from Suffolk, so I like to spend time there. In my spare time I swim and play Guitar Hero.

A Subprime Primer 2008
Client: Bad Idea
Magazine illustration; crayons.
© Jess Wilson

'This piece is about how banks have made money using ordinary people's mortgages. The text was supplied by the magazine's editors.'

A FEW WEEKS LATER, at the bank....

First Bank of
BANKLAND, USA

BANKER: I'D BETTER GET RID OF THESE CRAPPY MORTAGE LOANS. They're starting to stink out my OFFICE. THANKFULLY THE REALLY SMART GUYS IN NEW YORK WILL BUY THEM AND PERFORM THEIR "financial magic" I'LL GIVE THEM A CALL RIGHT NOW

Film Scripts 2003
Personal project; crayons.
Exhibited at 'Human Beings' at La Viande
in Shoreditch, and available on T-shirts by
T-bar in Australia.
© Jess Wilson

An ongoing project highlighting key funny
elements and emotions in a film, through
illustrated handwriting.'

JOE WILSON

What did you study?
Graphic Arts and Design at Leeds Metropolitan University.

What inspires you?
Science, natural history, astrophysics, surrealism, ancient Egypt, evolution, music and 1970s album-sleeve design.

What do you collect?
Old illustrated books of natural history, science and myths; the visual ideas and craftsmanship is amazing and something for me to aspire to.

What is your favourite way of working?
Nothing compares to working by hand with a pencil or pen, or creating a screen print and having a physical connection to that work. I like using all sorts of printing methods, such as etching and screen printing. But for everyday convenience, Fineliner pens, pencils and Biros are essential. I sketch rough ideas in pencil and rework in pen, improving as the piece develops. I scan them and use the computer to adjust and edit.

Where do you work, play and travel?
I work from a home studio and mix work with play. I like to travel to open plains and ragged woods.

The Bull and the Bear 2008
Private commission; hand-drawn, Fineliner pen, gouache.
© Joe Wilson

'An illustration on the subject of the bull and bear financial markets; the bull represents a strong market, the bear, a weak one.'

Blisters on My Fingers 2008
Personal project; B2-sized limited-edition screen print.
© Joe Wilson

'Contributed to an exhibition of 35 artists at "Blisters on My Fingers", at Print Club in London.'

Sun Giant 2008
Client: Mojo
Art director: Mark Wagstaff
Magazine illustration; hand-drawn,
Fineliner pen, Photoshop.
© Joe Wilson

'Full-page illustration accompanying
"Album of the month" by the band
Fleet Foxes. The loose brief was to imagine
"five human foxes in a medieval garden".'

Oscar Wilson/Studio Oscar

What did you study?
Graphic Communication and Printmaking at
Leeds Metropolitan University.

What inspires you?
My wife, family and friends; architecture, travel
and eBay.

What do you collect?
Mid-century modern prints, furniture and sculpture,
and disco records.

What is your favourite way of working?
Initially I hand-draw, then I rationalize the sketches
through multiple tracings, scan and clean them up using
a Mac. My favourite material is scalpel-cut Rubylith film,
and my favourite medium is screenprinting.

Where do you work, play and travel?
Work: London EC1. Play: on my bike. Travel: Tokyo
and New York City.

Stussy Hexstool 2007
Client: Stussy Japan
Furniture design: Ben Wilson
Self-assembly stool; laser-cut cardboard,
hand-screen printed.
© Oscar Wilson/Studio Oscar

'Having seen Ben Wilson's Chairfix,
made from MDF, Stussy Japan wanted a
product made in the UK. Because
of shipping, Ben needed to find a
lightweight material. Two identical
components are laser-cut from the strong,
recycled cardboard; they pop out of the
integral packaging sheet to slot together.
The hand-printed repeat pattern references
the hexagonal core of the material.'

1st Class 2002
Screen printing: K2 Screen; Vinyl: OMNI
Personal project; screen printing,
cut Rubylith film.
Shown at solo exhibitions at M&C Saatchi
and Tardis Gallery in London.
© Oscar Wilson/Studio Oscar

'Limited-edition prints and installation,
featuring a psychedelic portrait of the
Queen for her Golden Jubilee Anniversary.'

314

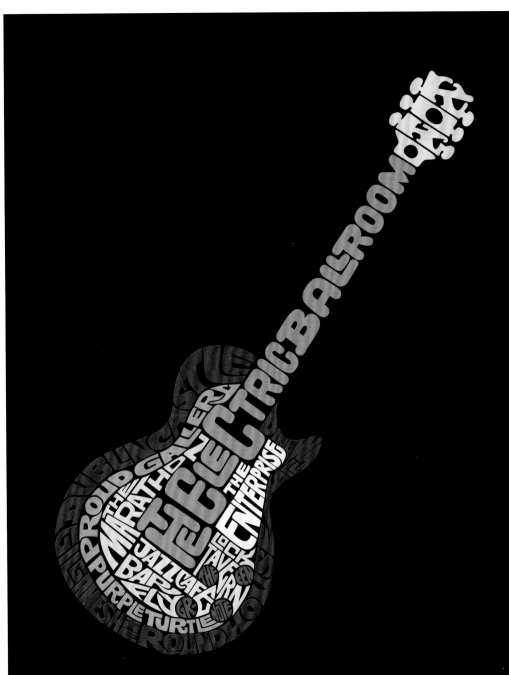

If you love live music
visitlondon.com/camden

Totally London 2007
Client: Visit London
Advertising agency: RKCR Y&R, London
Art director: Neil Durber
Copywriter: Ben Hartman
Advertising illustrations; hand-drawn,
Adobe Illustrator.
© Oscar Wilson/Studio Oscar

'A series of London attractions are
depicted typographically, starting with
a reference image. The copy is realized
through multiple redrawings.'

Steve Wilson

What did you study?

Illustration at the University of Brighton.

What inspires you?

Inspiration comes from a wide range of sources, including old record covers, Indian art, book shops, flea markets, 1960s psychedelia, 1970s rock posters, 1980s New York, music, and the pursuit of creating something better than I've created before.

What do you collect?

I regularly trawl the flea markets in Brighton and pick up out-of-print books with images that I can recycle, and a wide mix of stuff, which is reflected in the diversity of imagery I produce. I like the idea of finding things that no one else has that I can base my work on.

What is your favourite way of working?

It's so varied; in the last six months alone I've used children's liquid paint, woodwork, spray paint, Play-Doh, photocopiers, screenprinted textures, found images and all the obvious digital techniques, so it would be wrong to pick any specific method. I enjoy experimenting, and that I might discover a whole new way of working.

Where do you work, play and travel?

I work from home in Brighton. Lately, my favourite place to visit has been Morocco, especially Marrakech and the desert. In a relatively small area you can see sea, snow-capped mountains, desert and a completely different culture. That's the best kind of travel...when you go somewhere that gives you a completely new experience.

Sunbathe 2008
Personal project; Adobe Illustrator.
Collaborator: Corinna Radcliffe
Exhibited at 'Blisters on My Fingers' at Print Club in London.
© Steve Wilson

'Collaborating with Corinna, this is an attempt to incorporate pattern into my work.'

B 2008
Client: InkThis
Book illustration; wooden letter hand-dipped
in paint, photography, digital.
Published in InkThis 3, and exhibited in London.
© Steve Wilson

'A whole alphabet was created by different artists
and illustrators. I was given "B", and free reign.'

Bird 2008
Client: Island Records
Album packaging; Adobe Illustrator,
Photoshop.
© Steve Wilson

Bob Dylan 2007
Client: The Fader
Magazine illustration; handmade and found
textures, Adobe Illustrator, Photoshop.
© Steve Wilson

Sam Sparro 2008
Client: Island Records
Album packaging; liquid paint, paper,
photography, Photoshop.
© Steve Wilson

'Based on the artist's face, I illustrated this
image in an ironic way, influenced by the
1980s, futurism, nu-rave and the space
age, because this musician makes electro.'

Amy Winehouse 2007
Client: Vodafone
Advertising Agency: BBH
Advertising billboards; photography,
Adobe Illustrator, Photoshop.
© Steve Wilson

'Starting with a photograph of Amy Winehouse
performing live, the idea was to show her
tattoos coming to life, while incorporating the
information for the event, Vodafone's Live
Music Awards.'

What did you study?
Graphic Design at the Gerrit
Rietveld Academie, Amsterdam,
and Typography and Graphic Design
at the Royal Academy of Art,
The Hague.

What inspires you?
Recently, Bill Hicks.

What do you collect?
A lot of literature, books,
books, books.

What is your favourite way of working?
It changes on a daily basis, and I like
the diversity of the media I'm working
in. I hand-craft, by drawing, cutting
and painting.

Where do you work, play and travel?
Mexico!

Hardcore Rap 2008
Client: JFK
Magazine illustration; colour crayon,
pink paper.
© Job Wouters/Letman

'This shows the friction between American
gangster rap and its sweet nephew, Dutch
hip-hop.'

Amsterdam Weekly 2008
Client: Amsterdam Weekly
Cover illustration; Posca markers,
black paper.
© Job Wouters/Letman

'This issue was about Africa, so I decided to
make a Masai-inspired drawing.'

THIS IS

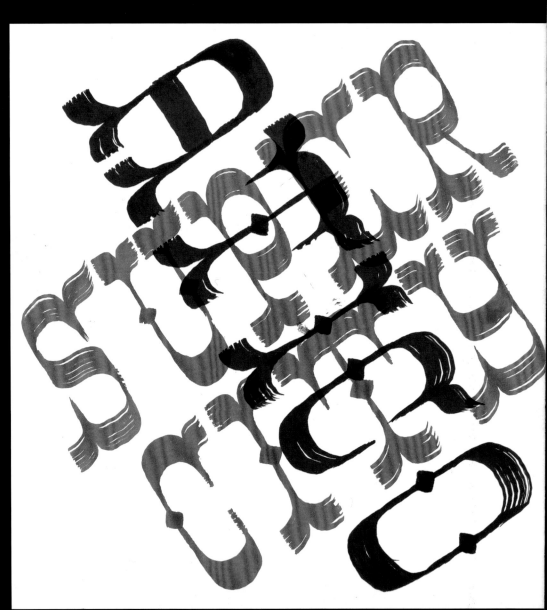

Supercity 2008
Client: Supercity
CD packaging; three-colour
stencil print.
© Job Wouters/Letman

'This limited-edition packaging
(1,000 were made) is for the
Mexican-Dutch band Supercity.'

VPRO Gids 2008
Client: VPRO Gids
Cover illustration; colour crayon,
grey paper.
© Job Wouters/Letman

'This was for the Dutch television
guide's travel issue and contains
a cryptic message; stack up the
countries and you can read in
Dutch, "fly less and read more".'

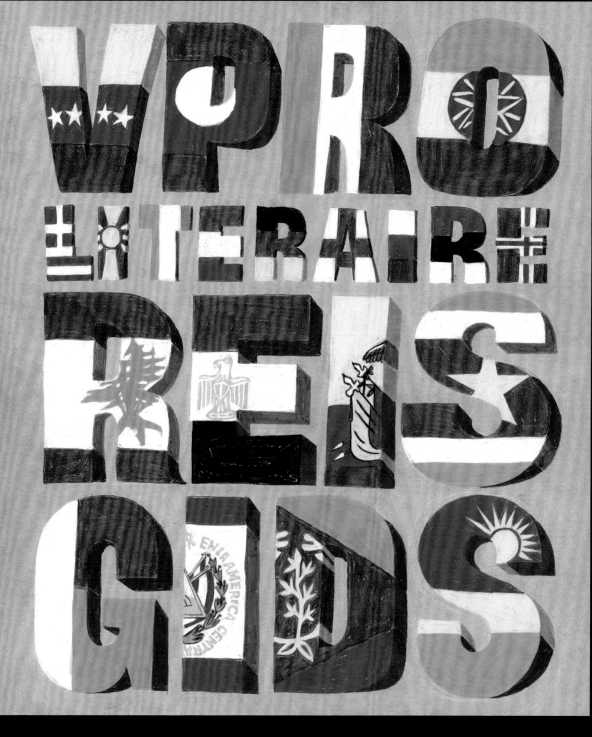

Contacts

Chrissie Abbott
chrissieabbott.co.uk
hello@chrissieabbott.co.uk

Eda Akaltun
edosatwork.com
me@edosatwork.com

Takayo Akiyama
takayon.com
info@takayon.com

Pablo Alfieri/Playful
pabloalfieri.com
pablo@pabloalfieri.com

Emily Alston/Emily Forgot
emilyforgot.co.uk
emily@emilyforgot.co.uk

Michele Angelo/Superexpresso
superexpresso.com
mike@superexpresso.com

Justine Ashbee
justineashbee.com
ashbee.justine@gmail.com

Jesse Auersalo
jesseauersalo.com
jesse@jesseauersalo.com

Clemens Baldermann/Purple Haze Studio
thepurplehaze.net
hello@thepurplehaze.net

Holly Birtles
hollybirtles.co.uk
hollybirtles@hotmail.co.uk

Pablo Bisoglio
pablobisoglio.com.ar
info@pablobisoglio.com.ar

Sebastian Bissinger/BANK™
bankassociates.de
sebastian@bankassociates.de

Laure Boer/BANK™
bankassociates.de
boer@banktm.de

Chris Bolton
chrisbolton.org
chris@chrisbolton.org

James Bourne
jbourne.co.uk
info@jbourne.co.uk

Paula Castro
senyoritapaula.com
srtapaula@yahoo.com

Ian Caulkett
iancaulkett.net
hello@iancaulkett.net

Pomme Chan
pommepomme.com
pomme.chan@gmail.com
hello@pommepomme.com

Johnny Cheuk
johnnycheuk.com
contact@johnnycheuk.com

Josh Clancy/Toothjuice
toothjuice.net
josh@toothjuice.net

Kathryn Dilego
hauntedhouseofprojects.com
info@hauntedhouseofprojects.com

Frank Dresmé/21bis
21bis.nl
frank@21bis.nl

Hampus Ericstam
hampusericstam.com
hi@graphic40000.com

Gary Fernández
garyfernandez.net
gary@garyfernandez.net

Ricardo Fumanal
ricardofumanal.com
info@ricardofumanal.com

Melvin Galapon
mynameismelvin.co.uk
mynameismelvin@gmail.com

Alina Günter
alinaguenter.ch
hello@alinaguenter.ch

Richard Hall/Listen04
listen04.co.uk
rich@listen04.co.uk

Sara Haraigue
lookatmedesign.com
saraharaigue@gmail.com

Sophie Henson
sophiehenson.com
sophiehenson@hotmail.co.uk

Richard Hogg
h099.com
richard@h099.com

Mario Hugo
loveworn.com
hello@loveworn.com

Christian Hundertmark/C100 Studio
c100studio.com
hello@c100studio.com

Marcus James
marcusjames.co.uk
marcus@marcusjames.co.uk

Zach Johnsen/Zenvironments
zenvironments.com
zach@zenvironments.com

James Joyce
one-fine-day.co.uk
james@one-fine-day.co.uk

Miki Kato
mikiart.blog39.fc2.com
mikimikimikikato@hotmail.com

Fernando Leal
fleal.com
fernando@fleal.com

Katharina Leuzinger/Mielo
katleuzinger.com
mail@katleuzinger.com

Anne-Pauline Mabire
annepauline.m.free.fr
anne.pauline.m@gmail.com

Harry Malt
harrymalt.com
harrymalt@mac.com

MASA
masa.com.ve
hello@masa.com.ve

Ivan Mayorquin
thejacksheridanblogshow.blogspot.com
quiendemoniosesjacksheridan@gmail.com

Átila Meireles
silencio.art.br
shhh@silencio.art.br

Gabriel Moreno
gabrielmoreno.com
gabriel@gabrielmoreno.com

Kate Moross
katemoross.com
kate@katemoross.com

Jarrik Muller/Get Busy Fok Lazy
getbusyfoklazy.nl
icanrollallday@hotmail.com

Pierre Nguyen
welcometocloud.com
hello@welcometocloud.com

**Oh Yeah Studio/Hans Christian Øren
and Christina Magnussen**
ohyeahstudio.no
post@ohyeahstudio.no

Sandrine Pagnoux
sandrinepagnoux.com
pagnoux@club-internet.fr

Sunil Pawar
slingshotlondon.co.uk
slingshotlondon@gmail.com

Mike Perry
midwestisbest.com
talktome@midwestisbest.com

Karina Petersen
karinapetersen.com
hello@karinapetersen.com

Lorenzo Petrantoni
lorenzopetrantoni.com
info@lorenzopetrantoni.com

Erin Petson
erinpetson.com
info@erinpetson.com

Qian Qian
q2design.com
q2design@gmail.com

Corinna Radcliffe
corinnaradcliffe.com
corinna@corinnaradcliffe.com

Revenge is Sweet
revengeissweet.org
info@revengeissweet.org

Janine Rewell
pekkafinland.com/janinerewell
pekka@pekkafinland.fi

Kerry Roper
youarebeautiful.co.uk
kerry@youarebeautiful.co.uk

Camille Rousseau
camillerousseau.com
camrousseau@gmail.com

Ryoono
ryoono.com
ryo@ryoono.com

Danny Sangra
dannysangra.com
dannysangra@gmail.com

Martin Satí
martinsati.com
martin@martinsati.com

Keith Scharwath
scharwath.com
keith@scharwath.com

Edvard Scott
edvardscott.com
me@edvardscott.com

Si Scott
siscottstudio.com
si@siscottstudio.com

Claire Scully
thequietrevolution.co.uk
claire@thequietrevolution.co.uk

Natsko Seki
natsko.com
mail@natsko.com

John Slade
john-slade.co.uk
john@hideyourtoys.net

Rose Stallard
rosestallard.com
rose@rosestallard.com

Staynice
staynice.nl
staynice@staynice.nl

Ian Stevenson
ianstevenson.co.uk
info@ianstevenson.co.uk

Sandra Suy
sandrasuy.com
hola@sandrasuy.com

**Toko/Eva Dijkstra
and Michael Lugmayr**
toko.nu
info@toko.nu

Alex Trochut
alextrochut.com
alex@alextrochut.com

UFEX
ufex.dk
info@ufex.dk

Antti Uotila
anttiuotila.com
auotila@gmail.com

Von/HelloVon
hellovon.com
say@hellovon.com

Ben Walker/benUFO
benufo.co.uk
ben@benufo.co.uk

Jarrett Webb/Obsolete Suite
obsoletesuite@gmail.com

Jess Wilson
jesswilson.co.uk
jswilson1984@hotmail.com

Joe Wilson
joe-wilson.com
info@joe-wilson.com

Oscar Wilson/Studio Oscar
studiooscar.com
info@studiooscar.com

Steve Wilson
wilson2000.com
steve@wilson2000.com

Job Wouters/Letman
letman.com
job@letman.com

Published in 2010 by
Laurence King Publishing Ltd
361–373 City Road
London EC1V 1LR
Tel +44 20 7841 6900
Fax +44 20 7841 6910
E-mail enquiries@laurenceking.com
www.laurenceking.com

A catalogue record for this book is available from
the British Library.

ISBN 978 1 85669 620 3

Designed by Start Creative

Printed in China

Thanks from the team.

Michael Dorrian
Thanks to Jo Pearce, Mike Curtis,
Darren Whittingham, Jade Barrett
and Andrew McGovern.

Liz Farrelly
Thanks to all the team for everyone's
expertise and patience; Olivia, Michael
and Lee at Breed and Start Creative and
Jo and Zoe at Laurence King Publishing.
Also to Helen Rush and Nicki Field at
Agency Rush, and Lawrence Zeegen for
chats. And always to Gregg Virostek.

Olivia Triggs
Thanks to the Breed artists; Paula Castro,
James Joyce, MASA, Rose Stallard, Si
Scott, Revenge is Sweet and Steven Wilson.
And to Jo and Zoe for their patience, and
a special thanks to Liz.

LAURENCE KING